WHAT'S YOUR AIM, KIM JONG-UN?

REVEALING HIS MOST RECENT THOUGHTS

RYUHO OKAWA

HS PRESS

Contents

Afterword

Preface

North Korea's young leader, Kim Jong-un, is currently in isolation. He cannot hold talks with the international community nor give his true thoughts.

His numerous missile launches and nuclear testing have brought out Mr. Trump's leadership skills, hidden the doubts of and extended the Abe administration, and allowed for China and America to become closer.

The new world history is about to flow quite differently from his scenario.

It would be like a dream if the mass media in the world, including Japan, were permitted to conduct a completely exclusive interview with Mr. Kim Jong-un now. Although a spiritual coverage, this book realized over 70% of that wish.

We have decided to put together and publish it right away to express the urgency of the coming D-day, while using caution to make sure it would not be used against us since he is a clever person.

Ryuho Okawa
Founder and CEO of Happy Science Group
Founder and President of the Happiness Realization Party
Oct. 12, 2017

What's Your Aim, Kim Jong-un?

Revealing His Most Recent Thoughts

Recorded Oct. 11, 2017
Special Lecture Hall, Happy Science,
Japan

Kim Jong-un (1983? - Present)

The third supreme leader of North Korea. The third son of previous General Secretary Kim Jong-il, he inherited the status of supreme leader after Kim Jong-il died in December 2011. Currently, he holds the titles of Chairman of the Workers' Party of Korea, Chairman of the State Affairs Commission of DPRK, and the Supreme Commander of the Korean People's Army, and so on.

Interviewers from Happy Science[*]:

Etsuo Ishikawa
Chairperson

Eiichi Satomura
Senior Managing Director
Public Relations and Marketing
Lecturer at Happy Science University

Taishu Sakai
Special Assistant to the Chairperson
Religious Affairs Headquarters

*The opinions of the spirit do not necessarily
reflect those of Happy Science Group.*

---

[*] Interviewers are listed in the order that they appear in the transcript. Their
professional titles represent their positions at the time of the interview.

1

Change in the True Feelings of the Dictator in the Final Stage of North Korean Affairs

The change seen in statements made by the Guardian spirit of Kim Jong-un on October 11

RYUHO OKAWA

The guardian spirit of North Korea's Kim Jong-un came to me again a short while ago and is with me since, so I have been wondering what I should do about this. We have already published a lot of books about him* and we pretty much know what he is saying, so I feel we don't have to publish any more spiritual messages from him.

Right now, in Japan, we are in the middle of a general election campaign for the House of Representatives.

---

* See *Kitachosen: Owari no Hajimari* (lit. North Korea: The Beginning of the End) (Tokyo: Happiness Realization Party, 2012), *Exposing North Korea's Menacing Leader: Kim Jong Un's Plot for a Psychological War* (New York: IRH Press, 2013), *Kitachosen Kim Jong-un wa Naze "Suibaku Jikken" wo Shita noka* (lit. Why Did North Korea's Kim Jong-un Execute Hydrogen Bomb Testing?) (Tokyo: IRH Press, 2016), *Kiki no Naka no Kitachosen Kim Jong-un no Shugorei Reigen* (lit. North Korea in Crisis A Spiritual Message from the Guardian Spirit of Kim Jong-un) (Tokyo: IRH Press, 2017), and *Donald Trump vs. Kim Jong-un: A Spiritual Battle between Two Leaders* (Tokyo: HS Press, 2017).

Yesterday [October 10, 2017] was the public declaration day, and October 22 will be the voting day. North Korea seems to want to do something, but the guardian spirit of Kim Jong-un said it would be bad if that influenced the outcome of Japan's election. He seemed to be concerned that political parties like Prime Minister Abe's and the Party of Hope would gain more seats if North Korea were to show threat. In general, he said he wants left-wing liberals to do better, so apparently, he can at least tell what would happen in that case.

I am not completely sure if it is a good thing or a bad thing for me to be a spokesperson for Kim Jong-un by publishing his spiritual messages. So, I was wondering what I should do. Our previous spiritual interview that we published was *Donald Trump vs. Kim Jong-un: A Spiritual Battle between Two Leaders* and both sides spoke fairly frankly in a head-to-head showdown. We recorded this in late August. After that, there was some progress and President Trump gradually grew silent, saying that it was "the calm before the storm." So, Kim Jong-un seems to have felt that Trump might be serious and is bracing himself well.

A short while ago, the guardian spirit of Kim Jong-un briefly mentioned something like, "If certain conditions are ensured, I could admit defeat," so I think he is trying to negotiate over the conditions.

Asking about the topics that we should listen to During a national election in critical times

RYUHO OKAWA

In any case, the national broadcasting station of North Korea cannot broadcast anything other than their usual, uplift-the-fighting-spirit announcements, so right now, Kim Jong-un apparently cannot talk with the international community. Because of that, while it is a bit strange, the guardian spirit of Kim Jong-un has come to Happy Science instead.

EIICHI SATOMURA

[*Laughs.*]

RYUHO OKAWA

I do not know if there is any merit for him to come to see us knowing that Happy Science might be the most hawkish toward North Korea. Actually, the Happiness Realization Party [HRP] would not have been established if it weren't for the threat of North Korea, so I guess we do have an obligation to see it through to the end. We have been taking quite a risk in warning about the threat of North Korea.

The guardian spirit of Kim Jong-un might be feeling a bit weak or lost. I feel that this might be the case. I hope we can dig into what he is thinking about during the election campaign and what he wants to do after that. Note that, since we are in the middle of an election, he might be thinking of stirring things up more or less. I'm not completely sure.

I think it is best to have the guardian spirit of Kim Jong-un speak as long as possible, so let's start this spiritual message. I would like for us to nail down the topics that we should listen to during the election period and decipher what he is trying to say. We have no reason to be admired by him so much, but it is true that he does not have anywhere else to turn to and he might be using us as a means to hold discussion with the West.

OK, then, I will summon him. [*To Satomura.*] You've interviewed the guardian spirit of Kim Jong-un before, right?

SATOMURA

Yes, I have.

RYUHO OKAWA

[*Claps once and puts hands together in prayer.*]

The guardian spirit of Kim Jong-un,
The supreme leader of North Korea,
Who has been with me since this morning.
The guardian spirit of Kim Jong-un.
Please descend to Happy Science
And reveal to us what is in your mind.
Thank you in advance.

[Approximately 10 seconds of silence.]

Spiritual Interview

2
How Does Kim Jong-un Analyze the Current Situation?

The guardian spirit of Kim Jong-un is Desperate for financial aid

KIM JONG-UN'S GUARDIAN SPIRIT
Hmm. Hmm, hmm. Hmm.

ETSUO ISHIKAWA
Good morning.

KIM JONG-UN'S G.S.
Hmm? Eh? What? Ah, yeah. Morning.

ISHIKAWA
Are you the guardian spirit of Kim Jong-un?

KIM JONG-UN'S G.S.
You forgot the honorific.

ISHIKAWA
Are you the guardian spirit of the supreme leader of the Workers' Party of Korea?

KIM JONG-UN'S G.S.
Yeah.

ISHIKAWA
Good morning.

KIM JONG-UN'S G.S.
Are you "Mr. Physical Manifestation" of the chairperson of Happy Science?

ISHIKAWA
Yes, I am.

KIM JONG-UN'S G.S.
Oh, OK.

ISHIKAWA
We heard that you have something to say to us today, but Japan is currently in the midst of an election...

KIM JONG-UN'S G.S.
Well, you should stop acting pointlessly.

ISHIKAWA
What do you mean by "acting pointlessly"?

KIM JONG-UN'S G.S.

It's a waste of money.

ISHIKAWA

Eh?

KIM JONG-UN'S G.S.

It's a waste of money to spend it on an election. So, send me that money instead.

ISHIKAWA

Ah, so you came to negotiate because you need money, right?

KIM JONG-UN'S G.S.

You know, it's probably not much fun for you when the mass media totally ignore you, right? Even after I launched 1, 2, 3, 4, 5, 6, 7, 8, 9, 10, 11, 12, 13, 14... 15 missiles this year to help you. The mass media don't even mention that the Happiness Realization Party has been warning against the threat of North Korea since 2009. The Japanese society is unfair. So, just give up already. You might be surprised just how much attention you could get if you gave that up and put forward a policy of using the election money to buy rice and oil, and ship those to us.

ISHIKAWA

In other words, you really are in need of funds now, aren't you?

KIM JONG-UN'S G.S.

Well, the thing is, you are trying to isolate us. And it is gradually taking effect.

ISHIKAWA

China's embargo seems to be rather effective as well.

KIM JONG-UN'S G.S.

Yeah, that, too. And our ambassadors are being expelled from many countries.

ISHIKAWA

Yes, that's true.

KIM JONG-UN'S G.S.

Those countries are putting pressure on us to withdraw, just like when Japan withdrew from the League of Nations before World War II. We might withdraw if things continue like this. You showed them that example, so isn't there anything that can be done?

How does Kim Jong-un regard his current situation?

ISHIKAWA

You probably do not have many options left, Chairman Kim. How do you regard the situation in which you now find yourself?

KIM JONG-UN'S G.S.

Trump is surprising sly.

ISHIKAWA

President Trump is tough, you know.

KIM JONG-UN'S G.S.

He's a sly old fox. I thought he was a little less serious.

ISHIKAWA

He recently expressed his resolve to "totally destroy" North Korea.

KIM JONG-UN'S G.S.

Hmm. They've been struck by hurricanes twice and there are wildfires in California. Isn't he in awe of the curse of God yet?

ISHIKAWA

He, himself, wants to implement God's justice, you see.

KIM JONG-UN'S G.S.

Hmm. Maybe North Korean agents are starting fires in California. It is really burning up, you know.

ISHIKAWA

Well, wildfires happen every year over there.

KIM JONG-UN'S G.S.

They are being attacked with fire and water, so maybe he ought to focus more on what is going on in his own country. "America First," right?

ISHIKAWA

Actually, public opinion in America is that he handled the hurricane situation well. People had predicted that, as president, he would not be up to the job, but in fact his popularity has increased. Apparently, they are now saying, "This man seems to be capable as a president."

KIM JONG-UN'S G.S.

As a democratic country, America has to take the mass media seriously, but he is being treated as a pariah and

"Kim Jong-unized" by them. How lonely for a president to only be able to tweet on Twitter . Don't you feel sorry for him? So, this pitiful American president needs to be assassinated or killed soon to put him out of his misery. He should stop "America First" and start "Me First" already.

ISHIKAWA
Your words seem to be less aggressive today.

KIM JONG-UN'S G.S.
Umm, your "halo" is overwhelming, you know?

ISHIKAWA
[*Laughs.*]

KIM JONG-UN'S G.S.
The light is blinding. There are two lights, so it's really bright. Hmm, what should I do? You know, your political party isn't going to win anyway. You should speak as an impartial observer and become our staff to serve as a bridge between Japan and North Korea. Then, you could attract international attention and succeed as a religion, too.

ISHIKAWA
Sure, we will try.

KIM JONG-UN'S G.S.
Isn't that right?

ISHIKAWA
Yes, that's fine.

KIM JONG-UN'S G.S.
You are an excellent example of a chairperson. You have the authority to make decisions. If what the chairperson of a religious group said are recorded, the group will just have to do as it is told.

Expressing his demands to the International community

ISHIKAWA
Could you tell us what you are asking for?

KIM JONG-UN'S G.S.
You know, the South Korean president talked about humanitarian aid, but he was made to retract that and now it's frozen. We are actually having trouble because nuclear development is costly.

ISHIKAWA

Aren't you spending too much on that?

KIM JONG-UN'S G.S.

No, no, I'm not. It is essential, so it's a necessary expense.

ISHIKAWA

Hmm.

KIM JONG-UN'S G.S.

We shouldn't drag the general populace into it. There are some Japanese amongst our citizens.

ISHIKAWA

I think you, Chairman Kim Jong-un, are the one who need to make an effort not to drag the general populace into it.

KIM JONG-UN'S G.S.

No, no, no, no. We...

ISHIKAWA

Your disposition to treat your people as pawns does of course mean that you cannot find common ground when negotiating with Western countries.

KIM JONG-UN'S G.S.

Nuclear development is something that has to be done from the perspective of Juche ideology* and military-first ideology. However, when it comes to other things, I think the international community should treat us with a little more love. As a religious group, shouldn't you be urging them to do that?

ISHIKAWA

Regarding that, Happy Science can serve as a conduit for you to negotiate with the international community.

KIM JONG-UN'S G.S.

Oh, is that so? Are you sure about serving as a conduit for negotiations?

ISHIKAWA

Yes, sure thing. In return, please let reporters from around the world into North Korea and show them what the country is like under your rule.

---

* The official state ideology of North Korea and Workers' Party of Korea created by the founder, Kim Il-sung. The ideology is an application of Marxism–Leninism to North Korea's reality which emphasizes that sovereignty rests with the Korean people and that a nation needs a strong military stance and national resources.

KIM JONG-UN'S G.S.

No thanks, I've had enough of the mass media.

ISHIKAWA

Our condition is that you show us just how happy your citizens really are.

KIM JONG-UN'S G.S.

We are showing that. Doesn't everyone look happy in front of the statues [of Kim Il-sung and Kim Jong-il]?

ISHIKAWA

No, simply showing us scenes in front of the statues is not good enough.

KIM JONG-UN'S G.S.

Men and women, old and young, gathered there yesterday [October 10] and were delighted to celebrate the anniversary of the Workers' Party. We showed footage of how happy they were.

ISHIKAWA

We have someone who is like a representative of the mass media here to ask you questions, so please hear his opinions as well.

KIM JONG-UN'S G.S.
Hmm, OK.

The "calm and measured" Japanese mass media Have no grasp of the situation

SATOMURA
In yesterday's celebrations of the founding of the Workers' Party of Korea, such as in front of the statues in Pyongyang, the usual...

KIM JONG-UN'S G.S.
Hey, why are you so suntanned?

SATOMURA
Ah, well, we're in the middle of an election, so I visit many places.

KIM JONG-UN'S G.S.
You know, someone like you [Satomura] in charge of PR who should be neutral and fair shouldn't be involved with elections.

SATOMURA

Actually, I am in fact making many trips to ensure a fair and neutral election.

KIM JONG-UN'S G.S.

Hmm. Well anyway, even if you guys maliciously try to stir up a belligerent mood toward North Korea, the Japanese mass media are "calm and measured," so they won't agree with you.

SATOMURA

What Mr. Ishikawa said just now is that we would really like you to let the "calm and measured" mass media report freely on the current situation in North Korea and see whether your citizens really are happy.

KIM JONG-UN'S G.S.

We are reporting it. Our citizens applaud enthusiastically every time a missile test succeeds.

ISHIKAWA

You only broadcast information that favors you [*laughs*].

KIM JONG-UN'S G.S.

What? No, that's not true.

ISHIKAWA

The people of the world have to be able to see for themselves.

KIM JONG-UN'S G.S.

My citizens all say, "Today, North Korea has become a powerful nation. We can crush America." So, they feel relieved. OK?

SATOMURA

You will find it very hard to gain the understanding of the global community with that kind of rather one-sided reporting. That is what Mr. Ishikawa has been saying. Regarding this, wouldn't you consider opening up a little and inviting the world to take a look at the actual situation? If there really are people in suffering, you could ask the global community for help.

KIM JONG-UN'S G.S.

You use the words "global community" too easily.

SATOMURA

Oh.

KIM JONG-UN'S G.S.

Abe and Trump are just making a lot of noise, instigated by Master Ryuho Okawa. America actually wants to practice "America First" and deal with domestic issues now, but Abe is deliberately bringing up the issue of North Korea and crying wolf, claiming that we are dangerous without a shred of proof. He dissolved the House of Representatives to hold an election to divert people's attention from his scandals. He is trying to win the election by making North Korea a scapegoat. So, you are being used with malicious intent. You really are.

ISHIKAWA

We are not being used with malicious intent, but rather...

KIM JONG-UN'S G.S.

Everything you do turns out to be opposite of what you intended.

ISHIKAWA

Yes.

KIM JONG-UN'S G.S.

So, you should say the opposite. If you launch a "We love North Korea" movement, it would produce the opposite results.

Japan should stick with pacifism To the day the world ends

ISHIKAWA

Are you, Chairman Kim Jong-un, positioned as a god in North Korea?

KIM JONG-UN'S G.S.

Huh? What are you trying to say? Positioned as a god...

ISHIKAWA

In other words, I am asking whether there is anyone above you.

KIM JONG-UN'S G.S.

I am a living god. What are you talking about?

ISHIKAWA

Oh, is that so?

KIM JONG-UN'S G.S.

Obviously.

ISHIKAWA

As for us, we believe that Master Ryuho Okawa decides the course we should take.

KIM JONG-UN'S G.S.

No, it's not true.

ISHIKAWA

He determines what justice is.

KIM JONG-UN'S G.S.

Your political party gets no recognition at all. However many lectures he gives, they are not covered on TV or in the newspapers, so it's completely pointless. I get instant coverage.

ISHIKAWA

Though you say so, when we started the session, you seemed to be dispirited.

KIM JONG-UN'S G.S.

I am a living god, like the pre-WWII Japanese emperor. The post-war emperor is just a decoration.

ISHIKAWA

The global community has been moving in the direction indicated by Master Ryuho Okawa since last year or so, and now, it's finally checkmate.

KIM JONG-UN'S G.S.

Well, it's because you guys encourage them. But you should think long and hard about the fact that doing so is not benefiting you.

ISHIKAWA

No, it's benefiting the entire world.

KIM JONG-UN'S G.S.

The more fuss you guys make, the stronger the Japanese left-wing liberals will become. The left wing will make huge strides in the next election [on Oct. 22]. If I show a little self-restraint and refrain from doing anything odd before polling day, I think the left wing will gain more votes. Abe and Koike [the former head of Party of Hope] have the same policy. Isn't that right?

ISHIKAWA

It is now 72 years since WWII ended and the post-war system is being summed up, so I think the left-wing liberals will finally be losing some power.

KIM JONG-UN'S G.S.

No, they will gain strength. They are getting stronger now. After all, you have to preserve Article 9 of the Japanese Constitution at all costs and keep Japan's pacifism forever.

"Japan will adhere to pacifism, will not possess military power, and will not fight a war." You have to stick with this to the day the world ends. Meanwhile, we will strengthen our military and fight against America and other aggressor nations. So, Asia will be peaceful if you provide us well with things like energy and food and become a country that supports us.

ISHIKAWA

Pacifism has been the national policy for 72 years, but with you building nuclear weapons and firing missiles, the Japanese people have realized that something needs to be done.

Japan should adopt the Juche ideology and Become a country capable of fighting America

KIM JONG-UN'S G.S.

Fundamentally, Japan really ought to adopt the Juche ideology, become independent, and become a country capable of fighting America, but...

ISHIKAWA

No, no. There is no need to fight America.

KIM JONG-UN'S G.S.

I mean, we were Japanese, too, for some time, not so long ago. There are currently as many as 130 U.S. bases in Japan, which essentially means it's an American colony, so movements like the one in Okinawa are right. According to Japanese history, a revolutionary movement always starts in the western part of the country, so you should expand the movement in Okinawa nationwide and launch a campaign to expel those 130 U.S. bases in one fell swoop, reassuring people that North Korea will protect Japan. You would win votes if you did that. Definitely.

ISHIKAWA

Now, things are moving in the opposite direction.

KIM JONG-UN'S G.S.

[*While tapping on the desk.*] You have no right to complain if you are attacked, given that you have 130 U.S. bases.

SATOMURA

Actually, sir, to be perfectly frank, the reason we have 130 U.S. bases is because the Korean War has not ended.

KIM JONG-UN'S G.S.

Hmm...

SATOMURA

The existence of North Korea does of course have a considerable effect. To give an extreme example, if North Korea and China were to become democratic countries, the deployment of U.S. bases and so on would completely change in the near future.

KIM JONG-UN'S G.S.

Due to biased media, most Japanese people might think that the U.S. bases in Okinawa are the only ones in Japan. They don't realize that there are others as well. There are 130 of them. You have to get rid of some. You have to cut down to just one or two. Yep.

3

Suggestions for a New Framework of Security in East Asia

Form a Japan-North Korea defensive alliance and Move nuclear weapons of North Korea over to Japan for protection

KIM JONG-UN'S G.S.

In return, since we possess nuclear weapons, we will move them to Japan and aim them across the Pacific. Then, Japan can be protected. We could probably cooperate like that. And if Russia were to make a move, we could protect Japan with our nuclear weapons. Don't you think we could form something like a Japan-North Korea defensive alliance now?

ISHIKAWA

If that were to happen, it surely would not bring happiness to the people of Japan, and neither would we be a country that can contribute to the world...

KIM JONG-UN'S G.S.

It would and you would be! After all, American soldiers would no longer be committing rape and other crimes, and there would be no more Osprey crashes. The Japanese people would be safer, and would no longer need to be complicit in all the bad things the Americans are going to do in Asia, or in the deaths of the huge number of people they would kill. If the Abe administration continues, Japan and America would jointly kill many Asians. You would be accomplices. In other words, you would be criminals.

ISHIKAWA

In our opinion, "human happiness" such as the freedom of the individual and the democracy we spoke of earlier does not exist in a world where we are protected by your nuclear weapons and missiles.

KIM JONG-UN'S G.S.

No, no, no. Without the government, the people cannot...

ISHIKAWA

There is no such thing as happiness in fear.

KIM JONG-UN'S G.S.

No, you have been brainwashed about that. You have been Americanized.

ISHIKAWA

No, we are not going to be brainwashed by you.

KIM JONG-UN'S G.S.

You're wrong. We are protecting the people with our nuclear weapons.

ISHIKAWA

Actually, what you are giving them is fear.

KIM JONG-UN'S G.S.

If it weren't for our nuclear weapons, America would build 130 bases in North Korea, just like they did in Japan. You know? We would be completely dominated. Virtually, you already... Your constitution was imposed on you by America, and they have bases throughout Japan. They have created a situation that prevents you from starting a revolution. So, you are in fact still a colony 72 years after the war, and you do not realize that because neither the mass media nor your government offices and politicians report that truth. *We* are the "liberation army."

Kim Jong-un's guardian spirit boasts that he will "Finish off America in one day"

ISHIKAWA

With regard to that, [the guardian spirit of] President Trump is now saying that it is probably about time that Japan had its own nuclear weapons as well, and is affirmative about Japan adopting a "self-help" attitude to defend itself, regardless of whether there are American bases here or not. So, the situation has changed completely.

KIM JONG-UN'S G.S.

That's because Mr. Trump is scared of North Korea. He's terrified that North Korea will hit Washington, D.C. with an ICBM [intercontinental ballistic missile]. He's terrified that the first-ever missile strike on America might occur during his presidency, so I think he wants Japan and North Korea to fight it out alone. He wants to avoid American soldiers being killed, as much as possible. It's "America First," after all.

ISHIKAWA

When the guardian spirit of President Trump talked about his plan, he said the fight with North Korea would be over in three days [Refer to the aforementioned *Donald Trump vs. Kim Jong-un: A Spiritual Battle between Two Leaders*].

KIM JONG-UN'S G.S.

[*Laughs.*] He's boasting, that's... We will finish it in a day. Yeah, in one day.

ISHIKAWA

President Trump might actually do it.

KIM JONG-UN'S G.S.

If we fire hydrogen bomb-tipped ICBMs and detonate them in the skies above Washington and New York, America would fail to function for six months or a year. Then, we can do whatever we want [*snickers*].

ISHIKAWA

This time, it's possible that America will take action before that happens.

KIM JONG-UN'S G.S.

Nobody in Japan listens to what you say, so I want to somehow remodel Japan for you. I won't hesitate to cooperate, you know?

Why the guardian spirit of Kim Jong-un came to Happy Science the day after the anniversary of the Founding of the Workers' Party of Korea

ISHIKAWA

By the way, is there some reason why you chose today to visit us?

KIM JONG-UN'S G.S.

Well, I thought you might be troubled because we didn't fire a missile yesterday. I thought you were probably disappointed because you might have thought it would have helped you in the election if we had fired a missile yesterday. To us, it's just like a firework show, you know?

ISHIKAWA

Ah.

KIM JONG-UN'S G.S.

You could do a lot of campaigns about it in the streets if North Korea did fire a missile, but the left wing would just get stronger if we don't, which is a problem for you, right? So, I just came to give a talk for you. Actually, we are prepared to fire one. We can fire them any time we want. The "fireworks" are ready. But I need to consider carefully before we do because it could benefit someone unexpected. That is what I'm thinking about.

Shaken by the rumor that the Chinese Communist Party's army will Invade North Korea

ISHIKAWA

The National Congress of the Communist Party of China will begin on October 18.

KIM JONG-UN'S G.S.

Yeah. It's somewhat troubling me at the moment.

ISHIKAWA

Ah.

KIM JONG-UN'S G.S.

A groundless rumor is going around that the Chinese Communist Party's army will invade North Korea. I think there is a very high chance that this is a psychological tactic, but just spreading such rumor leaves our people shaken. Our military is a bit shaken by it, too. If China invades, it means America and China would attack by pincer movement, which I would like to prevent. This rumor is going around, so I have to... You had better express your hatred of China a bit more directly.

SATOMURA
Is the North Korean army shaken by that rumor?

KIM JONG-UN'S G.S.
Ah, I'm just saying that there is such a rumor going round.

SATOMURA
Hmm.

"If Trump attacks North Korea, China will Beef up its armaments"

KIM JONG-UN'S G.S.
Xi Jinping does a lot of crazy things. Things he really shouldn't... He is putting on a front to look like a member of the global community although China must not be a country that keeps in step with America so much. China is actually completely different if you look under the surface. It's just like a bigger North Korea, you know? I think they are trying to use us as bait.

SATOMURA

Ah.

ISHIKAWA

So, you're going to be crushed by President Trump, after all...

KIM JONG-UN'S G.S.

No, if Trump attacks, what China will do is to beef up its armaments. It will put you guys at even more of a disadvantage.

ISHIKAWA

But if China jumped on the bandwagon, wouldn't your only options be to either use military force to preserve your political power or to flee to Russia?

KIM JONG-UN'S G.S.

Umm, you know, they are all fired up... [*Picks up a copy of* Donald Trump vs. Kim Jong-un: A Spiritual Battle between Two Leaders.] Trump seems to be coming on very strong... He probably doesn't have much time left. He'll probably die of a heart attack soon. I could probably give him a heart attack with just one blow. He comes on strong and says he can destroy North Korea in just three days, but if such a thing were to happen, what about China? China's economy is strong now and Chinese people are spending money in Japan and buying up land in various countries, but wouldn't it put you at a big disadvantage if China were forced to use the money to further develop its military strength for defense?

ISHIKAWA

That is the opposite way of thinking...

KIM JONG-UN'S G.S.

China would feel secure and wouldn't need to build up its equipment so much if North Korea were a country strong enough not to be threatened by America. You know?

What would Kim Jong-un do if the Chinese military were to flood into North Korea?

ISHIKAWA

I guess President Trump is thinking that China would learn to be somewhat humble if he takes this issue with North Korea to demonstrate the difference in military might. He is probably thinking the complete opposite as what you are thinking about.

KIM JONG-UN'S G.S.

But what about the hydrogen bombs, the H-bombs? We can't possibly miss if we aimed a hydrogen bomb-tipped missile at China. It's so close... America is a long way away, so we might miss our targets by a little bit, but if we aim at China... Imagine what would happen if a hydrogen bomb were to explode in Beijing. They wouldn't be able to intercept it. They don't have the ability to do that. It would cause tremendous damage. You know, if that were to happen, North Korea might be able to occupy China, given the right conditions, I mean.

ISHIKAWA

No, I don't think that is possible.

KIM JONG-UN'S G.S.

Umm, you never know, you know?

ISHIKAWA

The regime will collapse as soon as you decide to do so.

KIM JONG-UN'S G.S.

Actually, China could be knocked out with a single blow. Xi Jinping would be vaporized into steam and carbon dioxide by then.

SATOMURA

I'm sorry, but let me point this out. In the case of a democratic country like America, the government could change if a lot of people were killed by a hydrogen bomb, but in the case of Communist Party of China, the government wouldn't easily be threatened or overthrown, regardless of how many citizens die. So, comparing how many hydrogen bombs China has to that of North Korea, I think you would find it rather difficult to do. What do you think?

KIM JONG-UN'S G.S.

Hmm. Really? Now, I'm wondering what would be the most effective way to fight back if the Chinese military were to flood into North Korea...

SATOMURA

There hadn't been such great pressure on this matter in the past, but things are getting very tense...

ISHIKAWA

You wouldn't be able to fight back. So, don't you think it's finally time for you to relinquish the position of supreme leader?

KIM JONG-UN'S G.S.

Umm, well, I think it's just a threat. I think they are doing their best to threaten me and make me give up by saying that America will attack us with missiles and the Chinese ground forces will flood into North Korea. I have to think of some effective ways to fight back. I need to drag Japan into it more, so now, I have to somehow devise a new approach that takes advantage of Japan's political situation.

4

Confounded by U.S.-China Conformity, the Guardian Spirit of Kim Jong-un Speaks in a Liberal Way

Missile tests could be temporarily frozen, Depending on the international conditions

KIM JONG-UN'S G.S.

But you know, if your political party did make progress, it wouldn't be very good for us. Nothing good will come from that.

ISHIKAWA

But we would set up a table for negotiation, though.

KIM JONG-UN'S G.S.

I mean, it is true that Happy Science is our closest ally. But I also feel that you are the most hawkish.

ISHIKAWA

You could go into exile and survive.

KIM JONG-UN'S G.S.

Hmm...

ISHIKAWA

The only people showing you the correct choice right now are the HRP.

KIM JONG-UN'S G.S.

Well...

ISHIKAWA

China and President Trump are both taking this seriously.

KIM JONG-UN'S G.S.

So, if the international community can promise to keep the conditions that we might propose, then we could also agree to temporarily stop our nuclear program or temporarily freeze missile tests. But it depends on the conditions, you know?

ISHIKAWA

I don't think "temporarily" is a good thing.

KIM JONG-UN'S G.S.

Of course, temporarily... I mean, we cannot wait a whole year. So...

ISHIKAWA

Actually, "forever" is the condition.

KIM JONG-UN'S G.S.

No, that won't happen.

ISHIKAWA

Why not?

KIM JONG-UN'S G.S.

Because our idea of "forever" is one year at most.

ISHIKAWA

[*Smiles wryly.*]

SATOMURA

Oh, my.

KIM JONG-UN'S G.S.

It won't happen.

ISHIKAWA

I mean, it is true that the world has been tricked for about 25 years since 1993 [see Figure 1].

Figure 1.
In 1993, North Korea announced its withdrawal from the Non-Proliferation Treaty (NPT). In 1994, amid the rising tensions in the international community, former U.S. President Jimmy Carter (center of photo) visited North Korea to talk with President Kim Il-sung, and the country agreed to freeze its nuclear weapons program.

Beset on all sides, the guardian spirit of
Kim Jong-un is at a loss

KIM JONG-UN'S G.S.

You know, administrations change. And for Xi Jinping, now is the time that would determine whether or not he will continue to hold power. It's happening starting October 18, right? So, China also has its own politics to deal with. Things that could decide who the next leader will be. There could be changes in the political administrations of both China and Japan now, so it's somewhat difficult to make a move. Some people in China definitely have ideas that go against Xi Jinping's pro-U.S. thinking, so we have to bring those out to the surface.

SATOMURA

Ah...

KIM JONG-UN'S G.S.

Regarding that whole area, right now, I do have to think of some sort of military strategy. So... [*Clears throat.*]

ISHIKAWA

Your weakest point is that North Korea has little economic power. The relationship between the U.S. and China is not just about military power. President Trump has strong economic abilities, and the U.S. is using its economy as a weapon to put pressure on China, so there will be no escape for you this time. Things are already moving in that direction.

KIM JONG-UN'S G.S.

Hmm. You know, right now, there is Russia. We are working with them hoping for some sort of breakthrough. But Russia... It seems Happy Science is friends with Mr. Putin, too. You are a strange country. No, not a country. I mean, you are a strange...sometimes like a political party, sometimes like a religion. Putin, or Russia, seems to rely on you all as well, surprisingly.

ISHIKAWA

So, if you want to escape, we can let Mr. Putin know.

KIM JONG-UN'S G.S.

Umm, actually, I am still not sure about Russia. They might sell us out.

ISHIKAWA

They might sell you out?

KIM JONG-UN'S G.S.

Uh, yeah. They might. We cannot trust them too much yet because they might actually sell us out. But judging from how things are right now, it seems to me that they are not ready to get deeply involved to the point where they would fight against the U.S. or China for us. What should I do?

The guardian spirit of Kim Jong-un demands Liberal statements from Happy Science

SATOMURA

We have heard all sorts of opinions from you in the past. Judging from your conversation with Mr. Ishikawa today, it seems to me that you are trying to come up with an escape route with Japan, since President Trump placed a "bounty" on you, and China and Russia are gradually applying more pressure to win that bounty. Is this so?

KIM JONG-UN'S G.S.

Some sources tell me, "Trump is being very resolute based on Ryuho Okawa's opinion." It's having some impact on him. Some people say that the reason for Abe's highly hawkish attitude without grounds is due to your opinions.

So, you should do a 180 and say, "Poor North Korea. Stop bullying such a weak country." You could say that in your election campaign on the streets. "Don't bully North Korea."

ISHIKAWA
We actually do think, "Poor North Korea."

KIM JONG-UN'S G.S.
Right? So...

ISHIKAWA
We think that the 20 million people living under Chairman Kim Jong-un are to be pitied. That is why we are appealing to the world, hoping you would step down.

KIM JONG-UN'S G.S.
So, the current election campaign period is your chance to make your opinion heard.

ISHIKAWA
Yes, it is.

KIM JONG-UN'S G.S.
You know, your campaign on the streets? You [Satomura], your face is all red like a red demon, so if you say on

the streets, "Let us not attack poor North Korea!" then your hawkish image would completely change. If you work alongside the people who form movements to oppose the U.S. military bases in Okinawa and other areas and to oppose nuclear power plants, saying, "Let us protect our fellow Asians. No more American aggression!" then you might gain some votes.

SATOMURA

I see. However, as Mr. Ishikawa just said, the one who should do a 180 is not the Happiness Realization Party, but the North Korean side, which is to say you, Chairman Kim Jong-un. It is you who need to do a 180.

KIM JONG-UN'S G.S.

No, no, you can easily do a 180. You guys are a "totalitarian regime," so...

ISHIKAWA

We are a system of God's justice.

KIM JONG-UN'S G.S.

Umm, you know, if the chairperson [Ishikawa] really wanted to, he could immediately send us a mere 500,000 tons of rice, right?

ISHIKAWA

Umm... [*Laughs.*] Even if we sent 500,000 tons of rice, it would all just end up in your mouth and you would get fat. According to television reports and such, your citizens are all very skinny. As long as this regime continues, we cannot send rice to you.

KIM JONG-UN'S G.S.

Uh, so, you know? You could use Japan Self-Defense Forces [JSDF] helicopters. Instead of loading bombs, you could load rice bags, put parachutes on them, and drop them from the sky. We would hold off from shooting down the helicopters at those times. If you say you will do that, it would be a huge scoop.

ISHIKAWA

OK. We wouldn't mind doing that.

KIM JONG-UN'S G.S.

Oh, you don't mind? Your "OK" will be recorded here, you know?

ISHIKAWA

If we were to do that, then we would need to see your citizens actually get to eat it. We would need to have the mass media get in and do coverage there, and see if your citizens say it was delicious. We would need to ask that much as the conditions.

KIM JONG-UN'S G.S.

It seems Japan has a surplus of money. You have so much surplus that you have trouble finding ways to use it, right?

ISHIKAWA

No, actually, we are in deep financial deficit.

KIM JONG-UN'S G.S.

So, you should invest in North Korea's infrastructure maintenance. OK? You should invest in it.

ISHIKAWA

Japan invested quite a lot before WWII, too.

KIM JONG-UN'S G.S.

Umm, yeah, so you should do it again. I will allow you to do it. If you do it again and invest in us, we could become a country with bountiful industry and commerce. Then, you would virtually create a friendly nation in Asia, and there would be no threat. So, you have to come up with strong support and show goodwill first.

SATOMURA

No, I don't think so.

The U.S. and China are not supposed to team up

KIM JONG-UN'S G.S.

So, you should say, "We will support North Korea this much. From the perspective of a religion as well, the U.S. should not engage in any more invasions. Firing an ICBM from the other side of the Earth is going too far. Don't do something so absurd."

You need to say, "Guam was just stolen by the U.S. and turned into a colony." There is absolutely no legitimacy in their sending B1Bs or some kind of bombers, or whatever, from an Asian colony to attack North Korea. The U.S. is the one turning Asian countries into colonies, not us. Our nuclear weapons are purely defensive. A defensive measure in case the U.S. mounts an attack.

Japan does not have any nuclear weapons, so we are actually protecting Japan, in a way. If, by some chance, Japan were to be treated unfairly and were smashed and enslaved by the U.S., we could become the "liberation army" and come flooding in. Just give us money, then we can make more ships, more landing craft, and more tankers.

We want you to say, "Although things may be as they are, Japan is their old colonial master, so we will look after North Korea. We will negotiate everything in place of them." We want you to say, "The West should mind their own business.

Japan was invaded in WWII and suffered a great deal" and make sure we never see anything like that again.

The U.S. must not attack China. If the U.S. actually attacks North Korea, China might be next. If China were to team up with the U.S. now to defeat North Korea, they would be "getting their lips removed and exposing their teeth unprotected." So, they must never do that.

Considering this, Xi Jinping has to fall. I mean, he was steamrolled a lot by the U.S., both politically and diplomatically. He probably fell for a honey trap in Florida. No doubt about it. He must have been forced to sleep with a Florida beauty. Probably.

ISHIKAWA
Umm...

KIM JONG-UN'S G.S.
So, actually, I want Xi Jinping to fall this time. I want him to fall or maybe be assassinated. I want something like a "Xi Jinping decapitation plan" to be executed in China, if possible. Anyhow, the U.S. and China are not supposed to team up. OK?

ISHIKAWA
You are making quite a lot of complaint-like remarks today.

KIM JONG-UN'S G.S.

Umm, I just feel like my head is working very well today. I cannot help but think I have a military strategist's brains. I might be much smarter than Zhuge Liang*.

ISHIKAWA

Hmm.

Speaking of a North Korean-Japanese Military alliance and of liberating South Korea from the U.S. as a liberalist would

SATOMURA

What are the concessions you plan to propose to Mr. Ishikawa now in order to change the trend in the international community?

KIM JONG-UN'S G.S.

[*To Ishikawa.*] You are the chairperson, right? You should hold something that says "Chairperson of Happy Science" and stand in front of a broadcasting station with your feet

---

* Zhuge Liang (181-234) A genius strategist who was active during the Three Kingdoms period in China.

firmly planted there, like a gorilla. Say, "North Korea is a fellow Asian country. We are against U.S. nuclear strike on North Korea. It's absolutely unacceptable to destroy North Korea in three days. If that happens, Japan won't be able to get rid of a single U.S. military base. It will only result in more bases. It will only result in more across Asia."

You should say, "We need to send a supply of 500,000 tons of rice per month, petroleum, and other forms of energy. We should give free aid. Japan is already at zero or even negative interest rate right now, so we must not spend our money in the wrong way. That is why we should not invest in the Philippines or Vietnam, but instead invest in North Korea and solidify basic infrastructure there, so that North Korea can become a democratic nation. If that happens, they won't have to think about going to war, and if they can develop friendly ties with Japan, the U.S. will also understand that there is no need to fight." If you insist such points, even the NHK would have to broadcast what you are saying.

ISHIKAWA
Assuming I did that, what would you do?

KIM JONG-UN'S G.S.

Uh, what do you mean? Well, I guess I might say something like, "There is a decent person in Japan now."

ISHIKAWA

No, no, no. I mean, if I were to accept those terms, how would you change in return?

KIM JONG-UN'S G.S.

Umm, we will change our "North Korea First" policy so that we can form a U.S.-Japan military alliance or peace treaty...

SATOMURA

Do you mean U.S.-North Korea?

KIM JONG-UN'S G.S.

Ah, U.S.-North Korea... no, wait... no, no, no!

SATOMURA

Japan-North Korea?

KIM JONG-UN'S G.S.

No, I meant North Korea-Japan. Oops. We have to form a North Korea-Japan military alliance, and after that, liberate South Korea from American forces. We need to apply pressure toward liberating South Korea as well and, with a North Korea-Japan alliance, close in from both sides and remove American bases from South Korea. There might not be American Marines there, but they do have American military fighter jets and bomber jets, so we have to get rid of those.

Next, we definitely have to get those out of Guam. Make them retreat to Hawaii, and in the end, return Hawaii back to Japan, the previous owner*. We will help Japan fulfill the desire of taking Pearl Harbor in WWII, and since the Japanese people love Hawaii, we'll have America return it to Japan.

America should just cut down and plow through all the trees in the mountains of California to prevent brush fires there, build tons of nuclear shelters rather than colonies, and also build residential complexes. OK? They should just build nuclear shelters in preparation for an attack by North Korea. Yep.

ISHIKAWA

Umm, your proposals are quite far from negotiable [*laughs*].

---

* Hawaii was never under Japanese rule, but out of respect of the spirit's conscience, we have left his words as they were.

KIM JONG-UN'S G.S.

Really? But I think, if you say so, a lot of the Japanese mass media would agree with you because they are mostly left wing. It is a wonderful proposal. You would win a Nobel Peace Prize.

ISHIKAWA

Umm... Not a chance.

KIM JONG-UN'S G.S.

You need to teach the entire world about Happy Science, and win a Nobel Peace Prize. To that end, you need to claim strongly, "We will not let them fire nuclear missiles or drop nuclear bombs ever again in Asia." If you were to say Japan will be a shield to protect North Korea, I think everyone would be very moved.

The guardian spirit of Kim Jong-un says North Korea is being closed in ever since Trump appeared as president

ISHIKAWA

I wonder what you are really thinking. A while back, you, the guardian spirit of Chairman Kim Jong-un, came to Happy Science on Aug. 29 and had a showdown with the guardian spirit of President Trump [see *Donald Trump vs. Kim Jong-un: A Spiritual Battle between Two Leaders* as already cited]. At that time, you spoke very aggressively, but I do not feel that from you today. Is it true that you simply are very worried about what is happening? Are you out of moves?

KIM JONG-UN'S G.S.

Umm... You know, China changed its attitude to be friendly toward the U.S. all of a sudden, in just one or two months, which is just a little... I mean, this just cannot be... Hmm. Uh... Umm... It shouldn't be like this. Hmm. You know, what you have been teaching will end up in vain. That...

ISHIKAWA

[*Laughs.*] What will be in vain?

KIM JONG-UN'S G.S.

Your main concept. I mean, you know, you have put in a lot of effort into talking about the North Korean and Chinese threat the whole time in order to keep your political movement going. But China submitted to the U.S., doing as they are told. And if North Korea ends up getting defanged, there would be no threat. If so, I would be sad because you could be persecuted for your prophecies.

SATOMURA

No, no. Even a Japanese magazine published today has an essay saying things like Xi Jinping was skillfully manipulated in his dealings with Trump. It is true, however, that if Xi Jinping were to gain more power after the National Congress of the Communist Party of China that starts on Oct. 18, you would be in even more serious situation, right?

KIM JONG-UN'S G.S.

Umm... China would be losing out if... It should be a loss for them if North Korea were to be destroyed.

ISHIKAWA

So, it means they are thinking of a way to survive, even at such a cost. And this is because the current economic situation of China is worse than you think.

KIM JONG-UN'S G.S.

Hmm...

ISHIKAWA

Under the banner of "America First," President Trump is trying to pump mountains and mountains of funding into America, and so money from all over the world that used to flow into China is now all flowing into America instead, you see. And that makes things tough, even for a country like China. Things are really tough for them right now with this as a negotiation condition from America.

KIM JONG-UN'S G.S.

The Democratic Party and the American mass media are very strict on Russia, but Trump himself wants to have a good relationship with Putin of Russia. So, there is this strange thing going on where the mass media are trying to attack that. Meanwhile, Putin is thinking he could team up with Trump, so he is undecided, right?

ISHIKAWA

Hmm.

KIM JONG-UN'S G.S.

Yeah, so if Russia is really going to take America as a potential enemy and fight against them, then that's that. If the trend had continued from Obama to Hillary, then America would have been unified with the EU through the Ukrainian issue and would have taken the attitude to fight against Russia. Trump himself seems like he would do well with Putin. Abe is trying his best to get on Trump's and Putin's good side as if he has no pride. So, they are skillfully encircling us.

5

What Will Happen to the Regime of North Korea After Kim Jong-un?

Kim Jong-un's sister was appointed to an important Position to assert the availability of A legitimate successor

SATOMURA

You just spoke about the overseas situation and how you are being encircled. Another point is that you made a major change within your country—you promoted your sister [Ms. Kim Yo-Jong] to the virtually number two position of North Korea.

KIM JONG-UN'S G.S.

Hmm.

SATOMURA

This is a move we've never seen before from North Korea. I think this suggests that you appointed a direct family member as number two because you can no longer trust your closest aides. I believe this is how we should understand the situation. How is the internal situation?

KIM JONG-UN'S G.S.

Well, that is partly true, but with the assassination of Kim Jong-nam, some people are very angry. He has a son, Kim Han-sol, you know?

SATOMURA

Yes.

KIM JONG-UN'S G.S.

There are a lot of CIA-like schemes going on about breaking up the current regime and making the son, on behalf of his father, the top of a puppet state of North Korea, which may create a compromise between America and China and persuade the North Korean military as well as the Workers' Party of Korea.

SATOMURA

Yes.

KIM JONG-UN'S G.S.

They might be scheming that if they can have someone from North Korea rule the country as their puppet, they might be able to defang the party and the military by giving them hope that they will be able to survive as a country by simply replacing the head of the state.

ISHIKAWA

Hmm.

KIM JONG-UN'S G.S.

This is why I must put my sister there, just in case something like that happens.

SATOMURA

I see. So, it is to ensure a legitimate successor, right?

KIM JONG-UN'S G.S.

It is to show that there are still successors.

SATOMURA

OK. It's true that Kim Jong-nam had two wives, but as you mentioned earlier, one of his wives, and their son, are under protection in America.

KIM JONG-UN'S G.S.

Yeah. This is why I had Kim Jong-nam assassinated with VX gas the other day; I didn't want him becoming a puppet state leader.

SATOMURA

I see...

KIM JONG-UN'S G.S.

The assassination was successful. He even received money from America. He ended up receiving tens of millions, so it couldn't be helped that he was killed. I mean, he's pretty much a spy. I can't give the country to a spy, so I had him killed. It's a conspiracy. Since I used people from other countries, they cannot prove us guilty. Well, I don't know how the trial will go. I thought if I had him killed, they would not be able to establish a puppet state, but now they are trying to utilize his son. This information is also being spread. If they purposefully spread information stating that China is going to attack us or that the son of Jong-nam will succeed the top spot, our country will get stirred up.

SATOMURA

Ah!

KIM JONG-UN'S G.S.

I would have to kill him too, but right now, we cannot do anything to him.

SATOMURA

So, the assassination of Kim Jong-nam in February is now working in an unexpected way.

KIM JONG-UN'S G.S.

He's only a student, right? I didn't think that somebody was capable of being a successor at that age. But since I'm also young, maybe it's possible even if he is young.

ISHIKAWA

Actually, in international politics, America, China, and Russia are talking about what to do about the post-Kim Jong-un regime of North Korea.

KIM JONG-UN'S G.S.

Oh, yeah? Hmm, so yeah, that is the case.

At the House of Representatives election, The liberals should win

KIM JONG-UN'S G.S.

Japan still has some time in its elections. The Constitutional Democratic Party is popular among the mass media. If they are able to defeat Koike and if the LDP falls, Abe will also step down. With this, the Japanese Communist Party can grow, which will in effect pull Japan out from the U.S.-North Korean war. Japan should go back to its post-war attitude where you never take part in international conflicts. You know, the opposition parties strongly opposed to the conspiracy law.

SATOMURA

If that's the case, although this talk will be sidetracked a little, do you believe that for this Japanese election, the left or liberals, meaning the Constitutional Democratic Party or Communist Party, should win?

KIM JONG-UN'S G.S.

Well, if they can protect the constitution, Japan will no longer be a threat. We can just count out Japan.

SATOMURA

True.

KIM JONG-UN'S G.S.

You know, America has invaded Japan so much. If the mass media report on this fact, it will be apparent. If you start a new political party that takes the anti-American voice of Okinawa and spreads it throughout Japan, I think you will get a large number of votes.

SATOMURA

Then, for this election, those who vote for the liberals and left-wing ideals will in effect be supporting North Korea, correct?

KIM JONG-UN'S G.S.

No, that's not true. That would be rooting for international justice. This is the path toward earning a Nobel Peace Prize.

SATOMURA

[*Laughs.*]

KIM JONG-UN'S G.S.

This is the only path for you to earn a Nobel Peace Prize.

SATOMURA

That is what you believe to be international justice, right? I see.

KIM JONG-UN'S G.S.

Hmm, well, since you guys are working so hard for little reward, it's saddening to see all of your good policies stolen by Abe.

SATOMURA

No, just as Mr. Ishikawa mentioned earlier, we do not believe it's for little reward. We understand it as our efforts toward the peace and progress of the world. So, we definitely do not...

KIM JONG-UN'S G.S.

You put the precious donations offered from the believers into elections where the mass media ignore you. Isn't that a waste? Imagine if you take that money and change it to rice or oil to help out North Korea. You would see that as a religious organization, you will be standing out of the crowd internationally with your work. If you establish a neutral zone and bring it over to us in bulk, you would make a name.

The condition—
To keep the regime until 80 years old

ISHIKAWA

So, we would like to return back to the original point...

KIM JONG-UN'S G.S.

Your master is a savior, right? That's why he must save us.

ISHIKAWA

Are you, under this condition, thinking about stopping the development of nuclear weapons?

KIM JONG-UN'S G.S.

You know, my "stopping" means for a short moment. But I can say that I will stop. I've broken promises many times, anyway.

ISHIKAWA

Yes, we have been deceived for the past 25 years.

KIM JONG-UN'S G.S.

Yeah, well, hmm. So...

ISHIKAWA

How can the international community be guaranteed about that?

KIM JONG-UN'S G.S.

Umm, you should guarantee it then.

ISHIKAWA

No, we can't guarantee that [*laughs*].

KIM JONG-UN'S G.S.

You should just do a joint guarantee. Tell them that it was mentioned at the spiritual interview.

ISHIKAWA

No, that's not possible. Not even between you and us.

KIM JONG-UN'S G.S.

Umm, if Trump changes his mind, loses his standing, or if he dies, we can start again.

ISHIKAWA

Hmm. In the current situation, whether you will surrender or...

KIM JONG-UN'S G.S.

Here, I am negotiating on behalf of the ministry of foreign affairs. I want to see what you can give us to guarantee our survival in return for freezing our nuclear development on the surface and missile experiments for the time being.

ISHIKAWA

Hmm... We cannot negotiate on your terms.

KIM JONG-UN'S G.S.

Well, your ministry of foreign affairs is good-for-nothing. It's not even doing its job.

ISHIKAWA

The other day, Master Ryuho Okawa mentioned in his lecture that the message by Prime Minister Abe is correct. Prime Minister Abe said, "We have been tricked for the past 25 years by North Korea. We will not be tricked again. It's Chairman Kim who should change the policies." What do you think about this?

KIM JONG-UN'S G.S.

Umm, this was talked about during the first and second leaders, my grandfather and father.

ISHIKAWA

No, even you, the third leader...

KIM JONG-UN'S G.S.

I have not promised anything. That is a promise of my predecessors, and not mine. I am not them. So, they must make a promise with me. You know, America is having great trouble with hurricanes and wildfires right now. Also, a U.S. citizen shot hundreds of people to death. This is a national crisis, a terrible national crisis. They are in a national crisis, too. I don't want America to suffer further damage on top of such crisis. That's my love and mercy. This is why I advise them to concentrate on their domestic affairs and let Japan be responsible for Asia.

ISHIKAWA
Hmm...

KIM JONG-UN'S G.S.
Since Japan has an outstanding religion called Happy Science, they will be able to skillfully persuade everyone. You should just persuade like that.

SATOMURA
However, ironically, these national crises occurring in America are rather boosting the people's evaluations of the leadership of President Trump.

KIM JONG-UN'S G.S.
Hmm...

SATOMURA
We have been asking you to tell us what exactly you want in return for freezing missile experiments, stopping developing nuclear weapons or abandoning them.

KIM JONG-UN'S G.S.

Ah, keep the regime, of course.

SATOMURA

To keep the current regime under Chairman Kim Jong-un?

KIM JONG-UN'S G.S.

I want to keep going until I am about 80 years old, so I would like to keep this regime for another 45 years or so. Actually, 45 years is not a nice number. I would like a written promise to keep the current regime of North Korea for the next 50 years. So, they must talk about discarding the plan to eliminate the top members, and to guarantee that they will keep the Kim regime.

ISHIKAWA

America did not wish for the regime to change from the very beginning.

KIM JONG-UN'S G.S.

What?

ISHIKAWA

They have been mentioning for the past six months that they do not intend to change the regime.

KIM JONG-UN'S G.S.

America is full of liars, so you never know. You guys instigate them, you know? I don't know if they read the spiritual interview [refer to *Donald Trump vs. Kim Jong-un: A Spiritual Battle between Two Leaders*], but suddenly, America started to speak about "defeating" and that "there is only one choice."

ISHIKAWA

It's because you do not take the conditions, but develop nukes and launch missiles. This is why Mr. Trump thought it's no use and made a decision.

KIM JONG-UN'S G.S.

Well, the benefits that America will gain would be, "North Korea will not directly attack important cities like Washington D.C. or New York with nuclear weapons," "We will not conduct magnetic pulse attacks from nuclear explosions from the skies," or "We will not kill every single individual on Guam." With these conditions, it would be beneficial for them.

ISHIKAWA

[*Smiles wryly.*]

KIM JONG-UN'S G.S.

People in Guam are extremely scared. There will probably be no more tourists, since nobody knows when we will attack. Hawaii is also in danger. Next, nobody will go to Hawaii. Hawaii and Guam will both lose income.

SATOMURA

I believe these conditions are rather difficult.

KIM JONG-UN'S G.S.

You think so?

SATOMURA

Yes, for us to accept.

KIM JONG-UN'S G.S.

We are saying that we can refrain from launching a missile toward them. We are saying we will launch missiles toward and beyond the Sea of Japan. In other words, international waters that do not concern the U.S.

6

Kim Jong-un's True Thoughts behind His Japanese Liberal-style Claims

"We will not attack Japan as long as it observes Article 9 of the Japanese Constitution"

SATOMURA

You mentioned hydrogen bomb experiments in the Pacific.

ISHIKAWA

What are you planning to do next?

KIM JONG-UN'S G.S.

Hmm, as far as preparations, we did make a promise. We promised to launch four missiles toward Guam.

SATOMURA

I see.

KIM JONG-UN'S G.S.

We are ready, we can launch them at any time. Next, we have to show them something new, otherwise it's no fun, even for you guys. We find it necessary to show you that we can launch attacks from a submarine, and successfully attack American vessels on the Pacific side of Japan.

ISHIKAWA
Hmm.

KIM JONG-UN'S G.S.
In any case, we will launch missiles over Japan. But as long as Japan observes Article 9 of its constitution, we will not directly attack Japan. Here, we can be united, with the left-wing liberals of Japan. So, either Chairman Shii of the Japanese Communist Party or Edano from the Constitutional Democratic Party of Japan will finally become the Prime Minister.

ISHIKAWA
Hmm.

KIM JONG-UN'S G.S.
Both Abe and Koike from *Kibo no To* [Party of Hope] will have hostile policies toward North Korea. They may be trying to take away votes from left-wing parties by having two right-wing parties. If this is their strategy, this is not good. We are "friends" with Happy Science, you know?

Since we are friends, we still have some hope to change the situation through communications. At the very least, if I come to your master every night to beg him, you will listen to me since you are a religion, right?

ISHIKAWA

Well, we are just letting you talk.

KIM JONG-UN'S G.S.

Yeah. Or else, you won't be able to do any other work.

ISHIKAWA

This is why we believe that the time has come when you should rethink the contents of your plans.

KIM JONG-UN'S G.S.

Well, you must do what you must as a religion. America has dropped two nuclear bombs on Japan and heavily burnt down Tokyo with incendiary bombs. They are thinking about doing the same thing to North Korea. We would like you to speak out and say, "Asia should not be a test ground for nuclear weapons again. This should not be forgiven from a religious viewpoint." You still have about ten days until voting day, right? Try harder!

SATOMURA

We will make efforts to bring peace, even without your help. That aside, you mentioned that we must do what we must as a religion.

KIM JONG-UN'S G.S.

Yep I did.

SATOMURA

We hope that you will do what you must as a leader. For example, would you happen to be thinking about the option of stepping down in order to protect your people and maintain North Korea?

KIM JONG-UN'S G.S.

No, there is no need to do something pointless like that.

SATOMURA

Pointless?

KIM JONG-UN'S G.S.

Japan should just observe Article 9 of its constitution at all costs. As long as you keep this attitude, no one will attack you and...

SATOMURA

No, no. I am not talking about Japan, I am talking about you.

KIM JONG-UN'S G.S.

What?

SATOMURA

Would you happen to have the resolve to step down yourself or, in other words, to hand yourself over to the international community in order to break through the critical situation of North Korea and protect your people and country?

KIM JONG-UN'S G.S.

Umm, that is difficult. Just like how it is difficult for you to stay on a diet, I also have a difficult time dieting. I am unable to "shave off."

SATOMURA

Unable to shave off?

KIM JONG-UN'S G.S.

You understand, right? It's hard.

SATOMURA

No, I can.

KIM JONG-UN'S G.S.

I want to lose weight because my legs are injured, but I can't. You would eat if these gorgeous ladies served you food.

SATOMURA

You just cannot let go of your current status and lifestyle, right?

KIM JONG-UN'S G.S.

Of course, those would need to be maintained. Our regime is a monarchy ruled by me, an excellent or genius type person like an advent of God himself. A leader like me will not emerge through a democratic system. A hero cannot be born from democracy, unless there is somebody like me, who is born as a god, under the divine right of kings, you know? This is the best.

Insisting that North Korea with hydrogen bombs is Equal to permanent members of the UN Security Council

ISHIKAWA

If you try to declare these terms as you've mentioned today, you will end up admitting what Mr. Trump mentioned the other day, which was that "only one thing will work" against you.

KIM JONG-UN'S G.S.

Umm, Mr. Trump has not said anything specific about this.

ISHIKAWA

No, he hasn't.

KIM JONG-UN'S G.S.

Trump may be hoping that his death comes before the North Korean-American war starts.

ISHIKAWA

Hmm.

KIM JONG-UN'S G.S.

This "one thing" that he mentioned might be, "If I die, I will no longer have any responsibilities." It's possible.

ISHIKAWA

Mr. Trump believes he will realize the justice of God. He is not trying to keep a personal agenda, so he is strong.

KIM JONG-UN'S G.S.

But what he is thinking now is not compatible with "America First."

ISHIKAWA

America has the mission to realize the justice of God.

KIM JONG-UN'S G.S.

The U.S. has taken a lot of damage during the Vietnam War. They have aftereffects from this. Despite that, America is now trying to defend Vietnam from the threat of China. This seems totally absurd. Next, America will talk about nuclear attacks on North Korea, and then suddenly change attitude afterward. In future generations, they will probably say, unless they turn North Korea into a pro-U.S. country, they will not be able to confront the threats of China and Russia. This is why they must not go that far. You must dissuade them.

ISHIKAWA

I believe the biggest problem is not the problems of China or Russia, or the problems of the country. Rather, it is whether the citizens are truly happy under your rule.

KIM JONG-UN'S G.S.

Of course they are happy.

ISHIKAWA

You must know that God does not approve the current situation of North Korea, where people are not liberated and have no freedom.

KIM JONG-UN'S G.S.

Uh, I don't care about God.

ISHIKAWA

Umm, that's what really matters.

KIM JONG-UN'S G.S.

You know, only the permanent members of the UN Security Council have hydrogen bombs, so having hydrogen bombs means we are equal to them. To tell you the truth, I can do whatever I want to Japan. I can end your life at any time.

SATOMURA
Oh...

KIM JONG-UN'S G.S.
It is my mercy, like the mercy of Allah, that is keeping Japan alive.

ISHIKAWA
OK, OK. It has been decided that a regime where a dictator suppresses the people through force and fear is wrong.

KIM JONG-UN'S G.S.
No, that's not true. What Mr. Abe is doing is Nazism, just as you have been saying. We must defeat "Hitler," after all.

ISHIKAWA
Well, Mr. Abe only has about three years left, at most, in his political career. There is nothing to worry about.

KIM JONG-UN'S G.S.
Well, someone similar could appear.

ISHIKAWA
The Happiness Realization Party will make remarkable progress, so it's all right.

KIM JONG-UN'S G.S.

Uh, it doesn't seem like the HRP will make remarkable progress.

ISHIKAWA

Yes, we will.

KIM JONG-UN'S G.S.

I should just send in the special forces from North Korea and have them assault your candidates. This will make the news. Then, you will see some progress. Should I have them make an assault? They will just throw some *shurikens* [ninja stars] at the candidates.

SATOMURA

No, we won't need your help there.

KIM JONG-UN'S G.S.

If our forces defeat maybe two or three of your candidates, it'll be big news.

We will return one hundred Japanese abductees and Take Americans as hostages

SATOMURA

It seems like we are going around in circles. So, you are not thinking about abandoning nuclear weapons. You also do not have the will to stop missile tests. Neither do you want to guarantee, for the North Korea citizens, democracy, freedom or the right to believe in God.

KIM JONG-UN'S G.S.

It's what you guys preach. "Start by giving love." In other words, if you prove your friendship, there will be room to make some concessions on my part.

ISHIKAWA

And that is how Japan has been giving rice and other things to North Korea for 25 years.

KIM JONG-UN'S G.S.

Umm, that was in the past.

ISHIKAWA

We have continuously given.

KIM JONG-UN'S G.S.

You have not given us anything. Nothing. We have not received anything.

ISHIKAWA

We gave both rice and money.

KIM JONG-UN'S G.S.

A little bit in the 90s, but nothing after that.

ISHIKAWA

We gave pre-WWII, too. We made a lot of investments. However, we have been betrayed, over and over again.

KIM JONG-UN'S G.S.

You know, Moon Jae-in, the president of South Korea, will implement the "Sunshine Policy"* again to appeal and develop friendly ties with North Korea. They want to help the North Korean manufacturing industry make progress and send humanitarian support, too. However, they cannot due to pressures from the U.S. and Japan. This

---

* A policy to soften South Korean stance toward North Korea, first implemented by President Kim Dae-jung from 1998-2003, then again by President Roh Moo-hyun from 2003-2008. The policy has three basic principles: no armed provocation by North Korea will be tolerated, South Korea will make no attempt to absorb North Korea, and South Korea will promote mutual exchange and cooperation.

What's Your Aim, Kim Jong-un?

is serious intervention against the independence of the Korean Peninsula. It feels like a bad thing, like the Triple Intervention that was carried out against Japan.

SATOMURA

Honestly speaking, the past 25 years were 25 years of prolonged unhappiness for the citizens of North Korea.

KIM JONG-UN'S G.S.

Uh, you barely get any information coming in, so you shouldn't judge us like that.

SATOMURA

No, no. We have heard many stories from North Koreans who have run away.

KIM JONG-UN'S G.S.

All of them may be brainwashed. They are all being brainwashed by South Korea's KCIA [Korean Central Intelligence Agency].

SATOMURA

But there are more than 10,000 of them.

ISHIKAWA

If you say so, you should let the mass media from all over the world into North Korea and have them report what is happening in your country as well as your lifestyle. You need to disclose this information.

KIM JONG-UN'S G.S.

No, you guys should do proper paperwork and mention, "Under these conditions, we will come mediate." You want us to return the Japanese abductees, right? It's easy enough to return about a hundred of them.

SATOMURA

Easy enough?

KIM JONG-UN'S G.S.

Instead, we will take American hostages. Some Americans are reporting in North Korea, so we will take them as hostages. This is fine, we will return yours. So, the information we can provide would be to release some of the Japanese abductees, although they are quite old now.

He wants to protect peace in Asia from the U.S. by Having the left wing win the Japanese election?

SATOMURA

For more than 20 years, Master Ryuho Okawa has been saying, "For the sake of North Korea, they should open up and make a system to allow the media to report freely." It's been over 20 years.

KIM JONG-UN'S G.S.

You know, Mr. Trump is holding up even after people badmouth him so much. However, in my case, anybody who badmouths me, the leader, would be killed immediately. So, we must not disclose this information because if we do, my citizens would be killed. If they badmouth me, they would be killed immediately. By the following day, they wouldn't be alive; they would be floating down a river.

SATOMURA

Common sense in the international society calls that "an unfortunate condition."

KIM JONG-UN'S G.S.

Uh, China is similar.

SATOMURA

Yes, China is similar, but there is some struggle for power within the Chinese Communist Party. Their system does not allow for a dictator with absolute power.

KIM JONG-UN'S G.S.

Maybe so, but they have conquered many ethnic groups. We don't want to be like Inner Mongolia, Tibet or Uighur. That goes against our Juche ideology. My goal is to unify the Korean Peninsula, develop a brotherly alliance with Japan, and build up prosperity in Asia through our Juche ideology. This is justice. Japan is following America for more than 70 years, even after they killed so many Japanese people. You should be ashamed of that as an independent country.

SATOMURA

"We are aiming to become a nuclear state who can speak on equal terms with America. Since North Korea will guarantee the safety of Japan, Japan should cooperate with North Korea and support its current regime." Is this what you are thinking?

KIM JONG-UN'S G.S.

Japan's left wing must win the election. You should change your doctrines and prioritize the peace and independence of Asia instead of siding with America. Then, Ryuho Okawa would become the Gandhi of Japan and could win the Nobel Peace Prize. "North Korea, South Korea and China must not be attacked by America again. We will never let them attack Asia." Let us put up a barrier like this. Then, there will be a new relationship in power in the world. America should just think about themselves or ways to become friends with Mexico. They're mentioning about building a wall right now, right? They should get on friendlier terms with Mexico and get on friendly terms with Canada... You weren't able to go to Canada, right? Due to Abe's silly disbandment to hide suspicion in the time of impending war, Ryuho Okawa was not able to go to his lecture in Canada. I feel sorry for you. Of course, America should get friendlier with their southern and northern borders. They should use more energy there, since they are not on good terms. To not be on good terms with nearby countries means that America is a bad country.

SATOMURA

In foreign policy, there is a theory of cultivating relationships by getting friendly with distant countries while keeping somewhat antagonistic conditions with the countries nearby.

7
Kim Jong-un's G.S. Fears Losing North Korea

Where would he run to?

SATOMURA

Let me get back to the main point. You said many things, but I also heard that you might be willing to surrender under certain conditions. What do you propose?

KIM JONG-UN'S G.S.

Surrender is... I mean, there's "Surrender Science."*

SATOMURA

Umm, no. Please don't bring up our group name.

KIM JONG-UN'S G.S.

Eh? Aren't you going to surrender?

SATOMURA

No, we won't.

---

* Here, Kim Jong-un's G.S. is making a pun on the Japanese word kofuku, which can mean "surrender" or "happiness" depending on the Chinese characters used. Kofuku-no-Kagaku is the Japanese name for Happy Science, but he used it in the sense of "Surrender Science."

ISHIKAWA

In any case, it seems you have very few options at hand.

KIM JONG-UN'S G.S.

Uh, I do have an option. I just cannot see what will come after that.

ISHIKAWA

I would assume so.

KIM JONG-UN'S G.S.

I do have an option, of course.

SATOMURA

What kind of an option?

KIM JONG-UN'S G.S.

Umm, we could pull a surprise attack and deal some damage, just as you [Imperial Japanese Army] did in the past. But it's hard to see what we can do after that.

ISHIKAWA

The next time you attack, you will be totally destroyed. This is already set.

KIM JONG-UN'S G.S.

I guess you are asking me if I'm OK with the country being destroyed as long as we can deal great damage. Well, hmm...

ISHIKAWA

I guess China's betrayal or change in policy is quite effective.

KIM JONG-UN'S G.S.

The Chinese might support Xi Jinping's policy toward us, although it would likely be at a cost of many purges, but is that policy really good for them? Perhaps Russia and Japan would make a peace treaty, just as you say, and North Korea can get involved, so that we can defend ourselves.

SATOMURA

Some reports say that Russia has already established a defection route to Northern Europe for you and built a mansion to guarantee your life there.

KIM JONG-UN'S G.S.

Umm, I think that is disinformation.

SATOMURA

Oh?

KIM JONG-UN'S G.S.

They are trying to stir up our people. If the top flees, the subordinates will lose the resolve to fight.

ISHIKAWA

By the way, do you have any partner in the international community who would support your way of thinking?

KIM JONG-UN'S G.S.

Umm... Maybe Iran, since they would be the next target after we fall.

ISHIKAWA

I think the U.S. will announce another sanction against Iran, either today or tomorrow.

KIM JONG-UN'S G.S.

Iran probably wants North Korea to put up a good fight.

ISHIKAWA

Any others besides Iran?

KIM JONG-UN'S G.S.

Besides Iran, hmm... Bangladesh and Egypt. Also, I have connections in Switzerland. I could establish a government in exile if I could keep Switzerland from freezing my assets there. It's possible.

ISHIKAWA

It's sort of a poor country, whether it be Iran or Bangladesh.

KIM JONG-UN'S G.S.

Yeah, it's true. But if we fall, they will be the next targets for sure.

SATOMURA

This is the first time I've heard you talk about a government in exile in Switzerland.

KIM JONG-UN'S G.S.

I mean, I won't be able to act in foreign countries if my assets are frozen or confiscated. We've had connections with Switzerland from before. They are a neutral country. I have a lot of secret stash there, so if I can use those, I can continue my independence movement there.

ISHIKAWA

In your case, however, the world is keeping track of your money. You do not have the power to produce wealth by yourself in North Korea, and this is where they are attacking you.

KIM JONG-UN'S G.S.

What the U.S. can do next is to confiscate my personal assets and funds, and to restrict the freedom of movement, right? They won't permit these.

ISHIKAWA

The U.S. knowingly left those out in the previous UN resolution.

KIM JONG-UN'S G.S.

They knowingly... In short, they are trying to make me believe I can run away with my money.

ISHIKAWA

That's right. Economically speaking, President Trump is a god of prosperity, so he is very skilled in this matter. You've misjudged him. So, you cannot win this battle.

KIM JONG-UN'S G.S.

[*Clicks tongue.*]

ISHIKAWA

It's game over.

He is also considering firing nuclear missiles at the U.S. bases in Japan from their submarines

KIM JONG-UN'S G.S.

But if I lose, you won't have any work to do.

ISHIKAWA

In fact, we can do our work as a religion around the world.

SATOMURA

Rather, we want to get this issue over with as soon as possible in order to get on with our main work.

KIM JONG-UN'S G.S.

Umm, you are to be blamed for all the worthless books you published.

SATOMURA

You spoke those words yourself.

ISHIKAWA

Maybe you shouldn't call them worthless.

KIM JONG-UN'S G.S.

[*Shows the book*, Donald Trump vs. Kim Jong-un.] You are responsible for provoking. You are responsible for provoking a U.S.-North Korea showdown by publishing *Donald Trump vs. Kim Jong-un: A Spiritual Battle between Two Leaders.*

ISHIKAWA

We are letting people around the world know the true intentions behind this matter.

KIM JONG-UN'S G.S.

You can publish my words as books, but you should include a statement of apology, printed in bold letters, in the last ten pages or so: "Happy Science had been significantly mistaken on the way it dealt with and its opinions regarding North Korea." Then, have every mass media read that. You should say that you led the world in the wrong direction.

ISHIKAWA

We think that a leader of a country has the mission to realize the happiness of its citizens.

KIM JONG-UN'S G.S.

No, that's not true. The most superior one is standing as a leader right now, so if I were to die, North Korea would perish.

ISHIKAWA

No, the next regime has already been planned.

KIM JONG-UN'S G.S.

North Korea would perish.

ISHIKAWA

Kim Jong-nam's son might take the role.

KIM JONG-UN'S G.S.

Umm, do you think people would be happy with a puppet government under another country? If so, it would mean Manchukuo founded by Japan was right.

ISHIKAWA

Manchukuo was right.

KIM JONG-UN'S G.S.

No, it wasn't.

ISHIKAWA

Yes, the creation of Manchukuo was right.

KIM JONG-UN'S G.S.

Oh? If that were right, then what the U.S. did at that time [in World War II] would be bad, don't you think? What Mao Zedong did would be bad, too. Anyway, we have to keep peace in Asia, you know?

ISHIKAWA

Happy Science and the Happiness Realization Party will keep peace in Asia.

KIM JONG-UN'S G.S.

You know, you should demonstrate with the Japanese flag and supporting goods.

ISHIKAWA

We can do that, but in exchange, please open up your country.

KIM JONG-UN'S G.S.

If you send over tons of supporting goods on a treasure ship, then I'll tell my troops on the coast not to attack it.

ISHIKAWA

The world has a uniform understanding on this matter now. "We have been deceived for 25 years, so Chairman Kim should give first."

KIM JONG-UN'S G.S.

Uh, the one I trust the most now is Mr. Ryuho Okawa, and I believe he trusts me the most, too. You know? It would be utterly embarrassing if his spiritual messages were fake.

ISHIKAWA

We will surely convey to the whole world, what you said today. So, we are doing very genuine work as a religion.

KIM JONG-UN'S G.S.

You know, we *can* fire nuclear weapons. We can fire them in a real battle, not just as an experiment, and see how much damage we can deal, but it wouldn't be too good if we are to be destroyed because of that.

SATOMURA

Umm, we are not talking about eliminating North Korea. We are talking about getting rid of the current regime or the unhappiness of your citizens. So, ultimately, everything would really change if you changed the way you think.

KIM JONG-UN'S G.S.

You say so, but according to reports made by the U.S., they predict 2.1 million of their allies—South Koreans, Japanese and partially Americans—will die once the actual battle starts.[*] You have to think about what you can do to save those 2.1 million people. We can kill such number of people at the expense of being destroyed.

ISHIKAWA

What the world does not know yet is that there is an "attack" that wouldn't produce 2.1 million deaths.

KIM JONG-UN'S G.S.

At the least, we have a high chance of succeeding in our first strike, our preemptive attack. What would you do if I thought, "I don't care anymore" and made the resolve to fire a hydrogen bomb-tipped missile toward Marunouchi in Tokyo?

SATOMURA

Umm, I don't think you can at your current stage of development.

---

[*] 38 North, an American research institute on North Korea, stated its calculations on Oct 4, 2017, that a total of 2.1 million people will die if North Korea launched a nuclear attack on Tokyo and Seoul. The estimate is based on North Korea's nuclear counterattack assuming the U.S. military strikes North Korea first.

KIM JONG-UN'S G.S.

Do you really think you can shoot it down with PAC-3 interceptors?

SATOMURA

I mean, you cannot fire a hydrogen bomb at Japan yet.

KIM JONG-UN'S G.S.

Yes, yes, yes. It's possible.

SATOMURA

You've only recently succeeded in your nuclear experiment in North Korea.

KIM JONG-UN'S G.S.

Supposing I aimed the missiles at the Prime Minister's Official Residence, I don't think your self-defense forces would be able to shoot those down because the missiles are coming down from outer space, you know? Can they shoot those down?

SATOMURA

North Korea isn't powerful enough yet to deal critical and destructive damages as you say. So, you can still change now. Now is the time. You have to decide now. Now is the time to negotiate and change directions. Now is the time for you to change directions. You won't have the option to do so later on.

KIM JONG-UN'S G.S.

Well, I'm taking this positively. We have many bases on land, and the U.S. is planning to shoot at those places by taking satellite photos. So, I'm thinking of another experiment: attach a nuclear warhead on a missile and fire it from a submarine. Then, U.S. satellites won't know where it will come from. But this would only allow us to fire at close targets, so we can only deal damage to U.S. bases in Japan and whatever around those.

ISHIKAWA

But the U.S. forces have already done research on such attack.

KIM JONG-UN'S G.S.

Well, I don't think we would miss so easily.

ISHIKAWA

You might be able to start a small battle, but your country will definitely perish. In short, you are quite mistaken on what you think are major and minor matters. There is a huge gap between what you will do to satisfy yourself and what you will lose in exchange for doing so. I think it's time for you to make the wise decision and step down.

KIM JONG-UN'S G.S.

Umm, if that's the case, Happy Science should take a risk. You should say things like, "We will build a palace for Kim Jong-un in Japan and assign security troops to protect you, so please choose us as your place of exile," "We will protect you," "We will make sure to provide you with kimchee," or "We will guarantee you kimchee and yakiniku." Then, I'll think about it. I could go to Russia, but... well, Russia is dangerous. I don't know what they would do. They would kill people out of the blue.

SATOMURA

I see.

KIM JONG-UN'S G.S.

I'm a bit disappointed with China. Disappointed.

SATOMURA

Ah. Is that so?

KIM JONG-UN'S G.S.

Hmm. Trump, what a man. He is quite formidable, he can bring that Xi Jinping over to his side. Unbelievable.

How much time left until war begins?— "Ask Trump"

ISHIKAWA

What we want you to understand in this session is that the God of Earth has shown us, "Go in this direction" in terms of international politics. He has made His decision.

KIM JONG-UN'S G.S.

I guess things have been gradually shifting toward the direction that Ryuho Okawa is going, from around the U.S. presidential election last year.

ISHIKAWA

Yes, that's right.

KIM JONG-UN'S G.S.

You know, I want to do this in a mild way, so that you can... I want to let you take the credit.

SATOMURA

Umm, after hearing your opinions today, I got the feeling that, deep down, you are actually ready to completely surrender although your pride is keeping you from abandoning nuclear weapons and missiles.

KIM JONG-UN'S G.S.

So, you understand well that I'm a pacifist, right? I think you understand well that I strongly believe my citizens and I are one, and that the country would collapse if I were to disappear or be killed. You understand well that I'm protecting my citizens and that we are one. So, what can you do for me is...

ISHIKAWA

If you really are, then you should say directly to the international community, "I will discard this way of thinking, so please protect my 20 million people. I ask of you."

KIM JONG-UN'S G.S.

Umm, I would be killed if I were to prepare a script of the message and tried to have that broadcast.

ISHIKAWA

You mean, you would be killed by insurgents?

KIM JONG-UN'S G.S.

I would be killed by the military. We have some hawks in the military, so I would be killed by a coup d'état if I were to surrender.

TAISHU SAKAI

I assume you are wavering in your decision. Correct?

KIM JONG-UN'S G.S.

Yeah, I am.

SAKAI

How much time do you think you have left? I don't think the U.S. is planning to extend this much longer.

KIM JONG-UN'S G.S.

Uh, ask Mr. Trump about that.

SAKAI

You haven't read this?

KIM JONG-UN'S G.S.

Umm, how much Mr. Trump would...

SAKAI

Not a year or two, I would think.

KIM JONG-UN'S G.S.

Will he think about it after he sees the results of the Japanese elections and the Chinese congress, or will he think about it before that...

SATOMURA

President Trump is coming to Asia in the beginning of November.*

KIM JONG-UN'S G.S.

Ah, he is, so ask *him* why he's coming. We can fire a missile, but not if he's planning to make an all-out counterattack.

SATOMURA

You want us to ask him? So, it means you are aware that you are no longer in control.

KIM JONG-UN'S G.S.

Well, there is virtually no table for negotiations anymore. Secretary of Defense Tillerson is saying there is still a table for talks, but the president is saying there isn't.

---

*U.S. President Trump visited Japan, South Korea, China, Vietnam and the Philippines from November 5 to November 14, 2017.

SATOMURA

It's Secretary of State Tillerson.

KIM JONG-UN'S G.S.

Oh, secretary of state. Well, the president is saying there isn't. If the president says there isn't, then there isn't.

SATOMURA

So, you are saying this matter is so beyond your control that you cannot even make more time for negotiations.

KIM JONG-UN'S G.S.

Choe Son-hui, the director general of the North American department of our foreign ministry, went to Moscow to have talks with Russia. But apparently, she could not get any response that was favorable to us. So, a slightly better aid... would be all I need. But I don't think Russia wants to make an enemy of the U.S. since they are having conflicts with the EU. If push comes to shove, they would probably leave us to die.

SATOMURA

Ah. If a war were to actually begin, you would ultimately be killed, just like Hussein during the Iraq War. So, it has to be now.

KIM JONG-UN'S G.S.

I thought, "The military cannot kill me because the country could fall apart after that." But if a foreign power decides to install a puppet government and spreads the information in our country, our people would misunderstand and think that the country could still go on. Then, they might kill me. I think the CIA is working very hard right now too, trying to get people to fall under the illusion that as long as I'm removed, North Korea can maintain its current state...

SATOMURA

OK, OK, OK, OK.

KIM JONG-UN'S G.S.

But there is no way that the U.S. is thinking as such. There is absolutely no way that they are just thinking of killing me and keeping the status quo on other things. They certainly want to destroy our "military first" regime.

SATOMURA

All right.

KIM JONG-UN'S G.S.

Umm, you know, I cannot go with that. After all this, you...
You know, there is something called *gyaku-en** where those
who seemed to be enemies at first were in fact friends.
Don't you think this is us?

---

* A Buddhist term meaning "reverse opportunity." For example, one definition
would be, "slandering the Buddha could sometimes lead one to awaken to the
Truth."

8
Kim Jong-un's Final Aim—
Listing His Conditions

A "family meeting" was held in the Spirit World Where he received some criticism

SATOMURA

Now, I would like to ask you one last thing. Today, you have been talking in a very different manner compared to the previous interviews we had with you. So now, I would like to ask a question from a religious perspective.

KIM JONG-UN'S G.S.

OK.

SATOMURA

In our previous interviews, your grandfather Kim Il-sung and your father Kim Jong-il said they supported you.* We

---

* Refer to *Kitachosen Hokai e no Countdown Shodai Kokka Shuseki Kim Il-sung no Reigen* [literally, "Countdown to the Collapse of North Korea: Spiritual Interview with the First Leader Kim Il-sung"] (Tokyo: IRH Press, 2016) and *Kitachosen: Owari no Hajimari* [literally, "North Korea: The Beginning of the End"] (Tokyo: Happiness Realization Party, 2012).

also heard that Hitler visits you about once a week as your tutor.* What is their opinion over in the Spirit World?

KIM JONG-UN'S G.S.

You know, Kim Jong-il came this morning. Kim Jong-il, my father, seemed like he wanted to say something. Kim Jong-nam also came and tried to say something, but there's no way I'd let him. He won't say anything good nowadays. We are holding a "family meeting."

SATOMURA

I see.

KIM JONG-UN'S G.S.

But they're saying things like I'm "young and acting rash out of vigor." I need to be more cunning. Maybe I provoked too much? I think I did.

SATOMURA

I see. So, your family meeting is going in that direction?

---

* Refer to *Hitler-teki Shiten kara Kensho suru Sekai de Mottomo Kiken'na Dokusai-sha no Miwake-kata* [literally, "How to Distinguish the Most Dangerous Dictator in the World According to Hilter's View"] (Tokyo: IRH Press, 2016).

KIM JONG-UN'S G.S.

Hmm. The current election in Japan will finish in just 10 days. If Trump could hold off on attacking, the left wing wins, and Abe retreats, then the situation will change...

ISHIKAWA

That won't happen. The opposite could happen, but not that.

KIM JONG-UN'S G.S.

Hmm. Is that so? I heard the Constitutional Democratic Party* is becoming awfully popular.

SATOMURA

But they are running on only a small number of candidates. It's a tempest in a teapot.

ISHIKAWA

They are like the remains of the Kan administration that ruined Japan last time.

---

* A Japanese political party that was founded in early Oct. 2017, just before this spiritual interview. Its ideologies include preservation of Article 9 of the Japanese Constitution and opposition to nuclear power. In the 2017 House of Representatives election held on Oct. 22, the party won a total of 55 seats and became the leading opposition party.

KIM JONG-UN'S G.S.

Hmm. When a crisis occurs, it serves as a strong tailwind for Abe. Also, Trump is trying to let the Abe administration survive. So, it's hard to predict what will happen. If it gets out that Abe might lose the election, there is a possibility that America will meddle. If tensions rise, Abe will win, right?

SATOMURA

No, it's not guaranteed that Mr. Abe will win. Either way, you are undeniably cornered.

KIM JONG-UN'S G.S.

Hmm. Well, that is true.

SATOMURA

There will be the National Congress of the Communist Party of China from Oct. 18, Japan's election day on Oct. 22, and President Trump will visit Asia from Nov. 3. So, from what I see, I think everything will be decided during this time. Now may be the time to lay out your conditions to President Trump.

ISHIKAWA

We will try to notify what you said today to as many people throughout the world as possible.

KIM JONG-UN'S G.S.

I'm announcing through you guys that I am willing to negotiate the conditions.

ISHIKAWA

Hmm.

KIM JONG-UN'S G.S.

I'm saying through you that I am still willing to hold talks.

SATOMURA

I see.

KIM JONG-UN'S G.S.

OK? You guys can tell them not to be so hasty. I could freeze developments for a year, if you want. Maybe we can decide on the conditions during that time.

ISHIKAWA

But as we have been saying many times, we did this for 25 years. Yet, you continued to betray Japan and America.

KIM JONG-UN'S G.S.

In the past, that is.

ISHIKAWA

Mr. Trump said something like the presidents before him were tricked, but he won't be.

KIM JONG-UN'S G.S.

Hmm.

ISHIKAWA

In that meaning, unless you sincerely show what you will bring to the table, he will never come to the table of negotiations.

KIM JONG-UN'S G.S.

Maybe Mr. Trump will listen to "Great" Master Ryuho Okawa.

ISHIKAWA

Master Ryuho Okawa has already made his decision. He wants you to step down.

KIM JONG-UN'S G.S.

Uh, he should tell Mr. Trump to step down, too.

ISHIKAWA

No. Mr. Trump is currently trying to realize the justice of God.

KIM JONG-UN'S G.S.

You know, if your master is the God of the Earth, he should be saying, "Don't attack North Korea. If you nuke it, it would be the second Asian country to be done so following Japan, and would leave a bad mark in history that cannot be taken back." If he were the God of Japan, I guess he would not say so.

ISHIKAWA

Indeed, the God of the Earth is saying to you, "Step down like a man. It is the last chance to show your chivalry."

KIM JONG-UN'S G.S.

That means I won't be taking responsibility for my people.

ISHIKAWA

If you were to take responsibility for your people, you must be able to say, "I was wrong. The world will watch over your life, so please forgive me as I leave you" then disappear.

KIM JONG-UN'S G.S.

I do want to ask for wisdom from your guys, I mean, could you lend...

ISHIKAWA

This is our wisdom.

KIM JONG-UN'S G.S.

What kind of conditions, on your end, would allow me to maintain my pride and reach a settlement...

ISHIKAWA

Getting rid of your pride.

KIM JONG-UN'S G.S.

No, I can't do that. If politicians threw away their pride, then they would no longer...

SATOMURA

It means that voluntary retirement is still on the table. It's a possibility.

KIM JONG-UN'S G.S.

[*To Satomura.*] Voluntary retirement is something you will do. You look like my father and grandfather.

SATOMURA

No, no, no [*smiles wryly*]. It's still on the table for you.

KIM JONG-UN'S G.S.

If I retired at 34, I wouldn't have anything else to do.

SATOMURA

Umm, but there have been many cases like that throughout history.

KIM JONG-UN'S G.S.

I still have a lot I want to do for 40 or 50 more years.

SATOMURA

That's the biggest problem.

KIM JONG-UN'S G.S.

I'm young, so I'm still very motivated.

ISHIKAWA

But you have done so much in the first half of this lifetime. Isn't it enough?

KIM JONG-UN'S G.S.

Only a few years. My father died early and the people worried whether I was capable at the young age of 29. In order to wipe away everyone's fear, I was extremely aggressive, made the country bigger, and strengthened our military. I'd like to think that I am like Tokimune Hojo* who expelled the Mongol invasion.

SATOMURA

Really...

"If I should ever be murdered…"

SATOMURA

I've only heard this recently, but the first decade in the 2000s when Kim Jong-nam was still around, he told those around him that he was most afraid of Kim Jong-un tattling on him to their father. So, in that meaning, you've done enough...

KIM JONG-UN'S G.S.

Happy Science is a totalitarian regime like us. Why don't we just get along?

---

* Tokimune Hojo (1251-1284) The regent of the Kamakura shogunate, known for leading the Japanese forces against the two Mongol invasions. He was only 24 and 31 at the time of the invasions.

ISHIKAWA

No, we are not a totalitarian regime.

KIM JONG-UN'S G.S.

"Totalitarian alliance." If you make that call, 500,000 tons of rice should be delivered to us within a week.

ISHIKAWA

We can, but in order for that to happen, we are saying that you need to open up.

KIM JONG-UN'S G.S.

You could immediately send over 500,000 tons of rice by using a small portion of your funds. If you call upon your followers to donate to a "North Korea aid fund," you would immediately get the money. You know, I want to fire missiles, but one missile...

ISHIKAWA

It's quite costly.

KIM JONG-UN'S G.S.

Yeah, it is. A month's worth of food supply would disappear. So, we must fire them effectively.

ISHIKAWA

Your grandfather [Kim Il-sung] was quite worried.

KIM JONG-UN'S G.S.

We must not make any wasteful launches. Trump will come in November and try to talk about the post-war system, so before that, you should show the world that there are other options.

ISHIKAWA

Yes, yes, that's right. Mr. Trump advocates "America First," so he has been telling Japan to protect itself, too. This is how he thinks.

KIM JONG-UN'S G.S.

Ah, I don't care about that, but you guys must say, "May a disastrous nuclear weapon never hit Asia again."

ISHIKAWA

Yes, you are right.

KIM JONG-UN'S G.S.

All of Happy Science throughout Japan should recite a prayer like that.

ISHIKAWA

In order to do that, we need you to step down immediately. This is the best option to get rid of future worries.

KIM JONG-UN'S G.S.

Uh, I could step down, but my subordinates could get violent, you know?

ISHIKAWA

That won't happen.

KIM JONG-UN'S G.S.

I could actually be holding things down all by myself.

ISHIKAWA

You still have the most power as a dictator.

KIM JONG-UN'S G.S.

I can read the international situations more than anyone else can. My subordinates, not so much. So, if I should ever be murdered, the people may just want to say, "Let's carry out the will of comrade Kim Jong-un!" In that case, my sister may take over.

Listing the conditions for negotiations in The final phase

ISHIKAWA

There is one last thing that I'd like to confirm. Are you really thinking of stepping down if all of your conditions are met?

KIM JONG-UN'S G.S.

Hmm. I must be allowed to keep the current regime, guarantee my life and well-being. Do not nuke North Korea, do not attack us with the big bomb [Massive Ordnance Air Blast] that America dropped on Afghanistan, and do not interfere if South Korea or Japan wants to voluntarily aid North Korea. I need a covenant including all of the above that is under a joint signature by several trustworthy countries, otherwise I cannot say "yes" right away.

ISHIKAWA

What would you give up if all of those conditions were laid out on the table of negotiation?

KIM JONG-UN'S G.S.
Huh?

ISHIKAWA

What would you give up to the international community?

KIM JONG-UN'S G.S.

Like I said, I'll freeze my plans to totally destroy America.

ISHIKAWA

What are you going to do with your nukes and missiles?

KIM JONG-UN'S G.S.

Hmm. Well, I'm not sure whether America would come to manage them, China would come to manage them, Russia would come to manage them, or the UN would come to manage them. Either way, I need somewhere to go. As a last resort, a part of me says I could ride a nuke and be like a kamikaze squad. I want to leave my name in history, of course.

ISHIKAWA

OK, I understand. So, you are in serious trouble, right?

KIM JONG-UN'S G.S.

Umm, well, it kind of feels like something is "drawing near."

ISHIKAWA

Is that how you feel?

KIM JONG-UN'S G.S.

Hmm. At this rate, I mean.

ISHIKAWA

Your prediction is correct.

KIM JONG-UN'S G.S.

Hmm. I don't know if America's attack would already have started by the time Trump visits Asia, or if it will start then. I mean, I can fire a missile, but I cannot read how the situation will play out after that.

ISHIKAWA

All we can tell you is that it's time to step down.

KIM JONG-UN'S G.S.

There is no way I can step down. Not now.

ISHIKAWA

We will do our best to get this conversation spread around the world.

KIM JONG-UN'S G.S.

Hmm.

ISHIKAWA

Whether that will change the situation will depend on your luck.

KIM JONG-UN'S G.S.

You guys should change your opinion and say that the God of the Earth has changed his mind.

ISHIKAWA

That won't happen. He already made His decision.

KIM JONG-UN'S G.S.

The God of the Earth decided to protect North Korea...

ISHIKAWA

He has decided to protect North Korea's citizens. So, He is telling you to step down.

KIM JONG-UN'S G.S.

"If there is a nuclear war, more countries will come to possess nuclear weapons, so there must not be a nuclear war. America must not attack. North Korea is just defending themselves. As long as Japan upholds Article 9 of the Japanese Constitution, North Korea will not attack Japan." Can't we compromise on this?

ISHIKAWA

It is so hard for God to see 20 million people suffering.

KIM JONG-UN'S G.S.

Hmm. I haven't done anything so terrible. I'm just eating a little more than they are.

ISHIKAWA

Yes, yes, exactly. You give them fear and take away their freedom. You trap them in "Hell." This is unforgivable.

KIM JONG-UN'S G.S.

It's not Hell. It's not. We raise catfish in Pyongyang and use them as a source of protein, and we inspect how much rice we harvest.

ISHIKAWA

But I think recently, you set a strict rule that prohibited people from leaving Pyongyang for longer than a week.

KIM JONG-UN'S G.S.

You know, although I doubt it was broadcasted to you, a typhoon came to North Korea and damaged our crops last year. Now, we are nearing harvest time of the year, so if the fields were burnt down, it would be very troublesome. Even if it's not a nuke, a napalm bomb could burn our crops and cause us a lot of trouble. We would run out of food. We are afraid since we would run out of food.

SATOMURA

I see.

KIM JONG-UN'S G.S.

We cannot rule out the possibility that America would burn our rice fields like they did in Vietnam. They might be thinking that this method would bring less criticism from the international community. If they're thinking of disrupting our food supply, they may stop our imports from China and burn our rice fields. If this were the case, America would not be criticized as much because the international community won't understand what America is trying to do. They can say that they are not killing people.

His last statement: "Countries other than North Korea should adopt Article 9 of the Japanese Constitution"

ISHIKAWA

We are now approaching the end of our spiritual interview.

KIM JONG-UN'S G.S.

Ah, OK.

ISHIKAWA

Lastly, do you have a message to the international community?

KIM JONG-UN'S G.S.

All countries other than North Korea should adopt Article 9 of your constitution.

ISHIKAWA

[*Smiles wryly.*]

KIM JONG-UN'S G.S.

Especially America. As this constitution was given to Japan by America, I want them to adopt Article 9 and vow to observe "renunciation of military forces" and "denying the right to belligerency of the state," and to never again start a war by "trusting the peace-loving international community." Add Article 9 into the American constitution. In that case, I can feel at ease and continue to rule for about 45 more years.

ISHIKAWA

If this were to happen, North Korea must first adopt Article 9.

KIM JONG-UN'S G.S.

In North Korea, I am the constitution.

ISHIKAWA

If you want the world to adopt Article 9 of the Japanese Constitution, then North Korea must adopt it first.

KIM JONG-UN'S G.S.

I am for Japan's post-war regime that has continued up to now. It's a good regime.

ISHIKAWA

I understand clearly.

KIM JONG-UN'S G.S.

We could be a force in driving out the 130 American military bases located in Japan. The stronger the power of North Korea, the easier the negotiation will be for you. You should use that as backup. Today, I invited and talked to you as a window for negotiation or the representatives of the international community.

ISHIKAWA

OK. I understand.

KIM JONG-UN'S G.S.

So, read between the lines and really think about this. OK? You are not thinking about your party's interests and strategies, but are thinking about world peace, right?

ISHIKAWA

OK. It's time for you to step down, so please do your best.

KIM JONG-UN'S G.S.

Hmm. Well...

SATOMURA

OK. Thank you very much for today.

9

Ryuho Okawa's Simulation of Before and After D-day

The North's aim is to appeal to the pacifist Mass media in order to sap people's will to fight

RYUHO OKAWA

[*Claps three times.*] The tone of his words has changed greatly. This means that his last days are approaching. Kim Jong-un probably thought that if he bluffed, the opponents would be daunted. If he were dealing with parties like the U.S. Democratic Party and the Democratic Party of Japan, he may have been successful. However, America and Japan have become more hawk-like, so if they are pushed, they are more likely to push back strongly. On top of that, China may actually enforce sanctions on North Korea and Russia may not help North Korea.

ISHIKAWA

That is true.

RYUHO OKAWA

Russia probably doesn't want to become internationally isolated. Due to this, Russia might not have accepted to become a place of exile for Kim Jong-un. America has other moves they can make before they attack, for example, they can freeze North Korea's assets, leaving no way out whether North Korea likes it or not. By sheltering North Korea, China could lose trillions of yen in economic damage each year, which would be unbearable for China. If they were to be inflicted as much as three trillion yen worth of damage, China will just sell out Kim Jong-un.

SATOMURA
Yes.

RYUHO OKAWA
Of course, they will.

ISHIKAWA
Has that deal been settled?

RYUHO OKAWA
It seems so. What should Happy Science do? It seems like Kim Jong-un is asking for help from us, who are most hawk-like. What should we do?

SATOMURA
First, we should release the information as it is...

ISHIKAWA

And tell the world...

RYUHO OKAWA

But if we do that, we might be seen as "Kim Jong-un's Twitter." [*Laughs.*]

ISHIKAWA

[*Laughs.*]

RYUHO OKAWA

He probably won't be able to make this kind of statement on North Korea's national broadcast. When he speaks through it, he may have to say, "Enduring the unendurable and suffering what is insufferable" or "Well done, everyone," similar to Emperor Showa's Jewel Voice broadcast*. But he cannot find anyone reliable who will guarantee his life after that. If Kim Jong-un chooses not to fight, he may be killed by his people.

ISHIKAWA

Assassination...

---

* The radio broadcast in which Japanese Emperor Showa read out the Imperial Rescript on the Termination of the War, signifying Japan's unconditional surrender at the end of WWII, on Aug. 15, 1945.

RYUHO OKAWA

He has been the leader since he was about 29. His military probably wouldn't have followed him unless he was aggressive. If he pulls the trigger at the last moment, he may face a devastating attack. If he conducts a hydrogen bomb test, not in his own territory but in international waters such as the Pacific Ocean, he will surely be met with an all-out attack. He probably won't be able to bear it. Even if America were to attack in increments, North Korea could be devastated. We still remember Hussein [in the Iraq War].

SATOMURA

Yes.

RYUHO OKAWA

My prediction that we cannot play down President Trump was correct. We have already predicted this last year [refer to *The Trump Secret: Seeing Through the Past, Present, and Future of the New American President* (New York: IRH Press, 2017)]. With one more push, this may end without fighting. If they can finish this without fighting, I would be grateful. However, even if we have Kim Jong-un's words, I'm not sure if it's enough.

ISHIKAWA

There's not much that can be done...

RYUHO OKAWA

There really isn't much.

ISHIKAWA

However, publishing this interview at this time may have a big meaning.

RYUHO OKAWA

What is he [Kim Jong-un's guardian spirit] aiming for? Is he hoping that Japan will soften once the book is out? He is probably hoping that Japan's pacifism will grow stronger and will call off engaging in actual war.

SATOMURA

It seems somewhat so.

RYUHO OKAWA

Such way of thinking is quite common with the mass media. They might say, "If North Korea says they won't fire any more missiles, then let's leave it at that." They may try to sap the will to fight in this way. Or, if North Korea can remove sanctions from China, things may get a lot easier for them. China is probably ready to attack North Korea.

They may be trying to weaken Japan's political hawks

SATOMURA

In this interview, he was trying to take advantage of the Japanese election to boost his safety.

RYUHO OKAWA

Well, we cannot do anything about that. I'm not sure if we are being used, but the way to fight like the mass media do is to reveal the truth and let the people judge. If the subject is bad, just getting the truth out can lead to its breakdown. When Christian exorcists make a devil reveal its name, the fight is nearly over and the devil will leave the body of the possessed. Similarly, the moment you know someone's true intention, he or she could break down. Even if this ends without bloodshed, I don't think what we have been saying and fighting for will be for nothing. We are almost through with the most critical part.

SATOMURA

Yes.

RYUHO OKAWA

President Trump is a threat to Kim Jong-un as expected. If he wants to, he could make a move as if he went mad. This is indeed scary.

SATOMURA

What could not be changed for many years has finally changed.

RYUHO OKAWA

If this were President Obama, he probably wouldn't be able to attack, but would push for talks since he won the Nobel Peace Prize. Even if he were to ask North Korea to get rid of their nuclear weapons in the name of a "nuclear-free world," his words would bounce right back at him because he has nuclear weapons, too. He couldn't say that, for the American military bases also carry nuclear weapons.

It's uncertain whether we are being used or not, but I think he is running out of time, considering he came to me during the election period. He may be trying to soften Japan's political hawks.

Use our foresight beyond that of the mass media to Fight the information warfare

RYUHO OKAWA

What is our decision on this? It was the first time we saw Kim Jong-un's guardian spirit so shaken up.

SATOMURA

Yes. For the past couple of years...

RYUHO OKAWA

He was always so tough.

SATOMURA

He is almost completely encircled, both internationally and domestically.

RYUHO OKAWA

America has one more move in their option before going to an actual combat. It is to freeze North Korea's assets and to make them completely isolated from all countries. They are beginning to corner companies that do business with North Korea, but not to the full extent yet, right?

SATOMURA

Right.

RYUHO OKAWA

They are waiting for North Korea to give up and their submission moves seem to be working. Then, I wonder how things will turn out from now on. In Japan's House of Representatives election, I think if you put Mr. Abe's party and Ms. Koike's party together, they would make up more than half the total seats of the House of Representatives. Basically, I don't see Japan's direction changing too much. Even if the prime minister were to change from Mr. Abe to someone else, I don't think there would be a big change in the current. Supposing Mr. Fumio Kishida or Mr. Shigeru Ishiba [of the Liberal Democratic Party] were to come out, I don't think they would be able to oppose America's opinions. So, I think the end result will be the same. South Korea's President Moon might already be disregarded by America.

SATOMURA

That is true.

RYUHO OKAWA

He did not want to introduce the THAAD [Terminal High Altitude Area Defense] system, but was forced to do so.

SATOMURA

Yes.

The end is near

RYUHO OKAWA

Anyway, the end is near. All that is left is to see if President Trump will corner North Korea even further, without letting them off the hook. If they are still on alert after the hurricanes, brush fires, and shooting rampage, then this could end. It is near. Three aircraft carriers are in one area, so they won't be able to take America on.

ISHIKAWA

The aircraft carriers are nearby, so yes.

RYUHO OKAWA

They could even attack North Korea's submarines. Even the Japanese Air Self-Defense Force and the Maritime Self-Defense Force could sink a submarine. All we can do is to have people know the truth with this spiritual interview. We must let them know that the currents have changed. It was good that Happy Science supported Mr. Trump last year. We have more foresight than the mass media.

SATOMURA

Indeed.

RYUHO OKAWA

CNN is still attacking President Trump. Happy Science has mass media-like capabilities, too. There are also battles using words, so we would like people to use our statements in information warfare.

INTERVIEWERS

Thank you very much.

Afterword

We must not yet drop our guard by trusting his words alone. There is no saying what a person, in order to preserve his physical life on earth, who is combative, will do when cornered.

Even so, the words of Kim Jong-un's guardian spirit in this book help clarify, in return, the status quo of Japanese politics for sure.

The appearance of President Trump and the extended administration of Prime Minister Abe, who is quite different from the traditional Liberal Democratic Party leaders, after his return—these two were necessary events in history, and people made the correct choice on this point.

We cannot be sure if we managed to fully accomplish our mission in history. But although we may not appear to be a hero in the public eye, if we can work as the "Dark Knight" to save many lives, as well as give people "freedom from fear," I think those alone are good enough.

Ryuho Okawa
Founder and CEO of Happy Science Group
Founder and President of the Happiness Realization Party
Oct. 12, 2017

ABOUT THE AUTHOR

Founder and CEO of Happy Science Group.

Ryuho Okawa was born on July 7th 1956, in Tokushima, Japan. After graduating from the University of Tokyo with a law degree, he joined a Tokyo-based trading house. While working at its New York headquarters, he studied international finance at the Graduate Center of the City University of New York. In 1981, he attained Great Enlightenment and became aware that he is El Cantare with a mission to bring salvation to all humankind.

In 1986, he established Happy Science. It now has members in over 165 countries across the world, with more than 700 branches and temples as well as 10,000 missionary houses around the world.

He has given over 3,400 lectures (of which more than 150 are in English) and published over 3,000 books (of which more than 600 are Spiritual Interview Series), and many are translated into 40 languages. Along with *The Laws of the Sun* and *The Laws Of Messiah*, many of the books have become best sellers or million sellers. To date, Happy Science has produced 25 movies. The original story and original concept were given by the Executive Producer Ryuho Okawa. He has also composed music and written lyrics of over 450 pieces.

Moreover, he is the Founder of Happy Science University and Happy Science Academy (Junior and Senior High School), Founder and President of the Happiness Realization Party, Founder and Honorary Headmaster of Happy Science Institute of Government and Management, Founder of IRH Press Co., Ltd., and the Chairperson of NEW STAR PRODUCTION Co., Ltd. and ARI Production Co., Ltd.

WHAT IS EL CANTARE?

El Cantare means "the Light of the Earth," and is the Supreme God of the Earth who has been guiding humankind since the beginning of Genesis. He is whom Jesus called Father and Muhammad called Allah, and is *Ame-no-Mioya-Gami*, Japanese Father God. Different parts of El Cantare's core consciousness have descended to Earth in the past, once as Alpha and another as Elohim. His branch spirits, such as Shakyamuni Buddha and Hermes, have descended to Earth many times and helped to flourish many civilizations. To unite various religions and to integrate various fields of study in order to build a new civilization on Earth, a part of the core consciousness has descended to Earth as Master Ryuho Okawa.

Alpha is a part of the core consciousness of El Cantare who descended to Earth around 330 million years ago. Alpha preached Earth's Truths to harmonize and unify Earth-born humans and space people who came from other planets.

Elohim is a part of El Cantare's core consciousness who descended to Earth around 150 million years ago. He gave wisdom, mainly on the differences of light and darkness, good and evil.

Ame-no-Mioya-Gami (Japanese Father God) is the Creator God and the Father God who appears in the ancient literature, *Hotsuma Tsutae*. It is believed that He descended on the foothills of Mt. Fuji about 30,000 years ago and built the Fuji dynasty, which is the root of the Japanese civilization. With justice as the central pillar, Ame-no-Mioya-Gami's teachings spread to ancient civilizations of other countries in the world.

Shakyamuni Buddha was born as a prince into the Shakya Clan in India around 2,600 years ago. When he was 29 years old, he renounced the world and sought enlightenment. He later attained Great Enlightenment and founded Buddhism.

Hermes is one of the 12 Olympian gods in Greek mythology, but the spiritual Truth is that he taught the teachings of love and progress around 4,300 years ago that became the origin of the current Western civilization. He is a hero that truly existed.

Ophealis was born in Greece around 6,500 years ago and was the leader who took an expedition to as far as Egypt. He is the God of miracles, prosperity, and arts, and is known as Osiris in the Egyptian mythology.

Rient Arl Croud was born as a king of the ancient Incan Empire around 7,000 years ago and taught about the mysteries of the mind. In the heavenly world, he is responsible for the interactions that take place between various planets.

Thoth was an almighty leader who built the golden age of the Atlantic civilization around 12,000 years ago. In the Egyptian mythology, he is known as god Thoth.

Ra Mu was a leader who built the golden age of the civilization of Mu around 17,000 years ago. As a religious leader and a politician, he ruled by uniting religion and politics.

WHAT IS A SPIRITUAL MESSAGE?

We are all spiritual beings living on this earth. The following is the mechanism behind Master Ryuho Okawa's spiritual messages.

1 You are a spirit

People are born into this world to gain wisdom through various experiences and return to the other world when their lives end. We are all spirits and repeat this cycle in order to refine our souls.

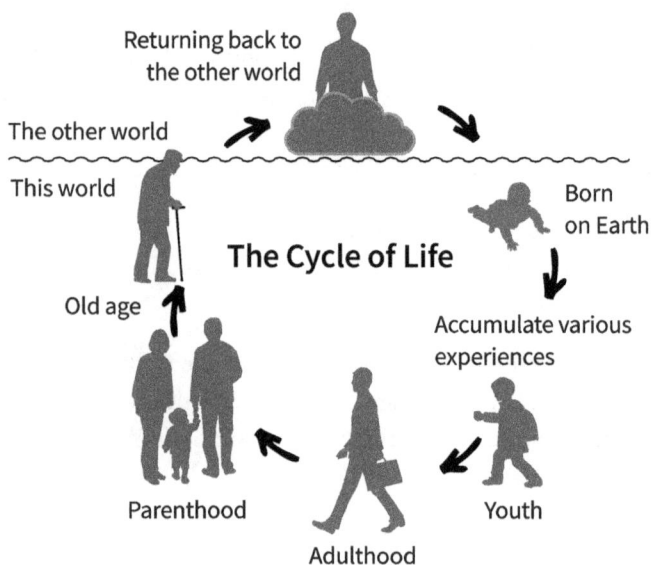

Returning back to
the other world

The other world

This world

Born
on Earth

Old age

The Cycle of Life

Accumulate various
experiences

Parenthood

Adulthood

Youth

2 You have a guardian spirit

Guardian spirits are those who protect the people who are living on this earth. Each of us has a guardian spirit that watches over us and guides us from the other world. They were us in our past life, and are identical in how we think.

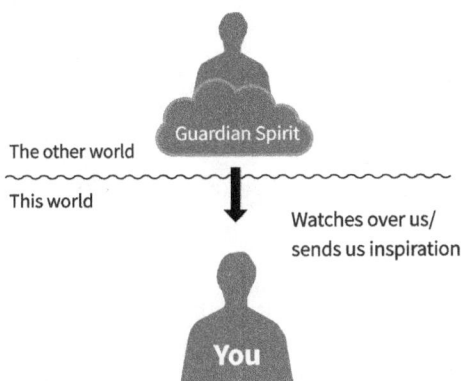

The other world

This world

Guardian Spirit

Watches over us/
sends us inspiration

You

3 How spiritual messages work

Master Ryuho Okawa, through his enlightenment, is capable of summoning any spirit from anywhere in the world, including the spirit world.

Master Okawa's way of receiving spiritual messages is fundamentally different from that of other psychic mediums who undergo trances and are thereby completely taken over by the spirits they are channeling.

Master Okawa's attainment of a high level of enlightenment enables him to retain full control of his consciousness and body throughout the duration of the spiritual message. To allow the spirits to express their own thoughts and personalities freely, however, Master Okawa usually softens the dominancy of his consciousness. This way, he is able to keep his own philosophies out of the way and ensure that the spiritual messages are pure expressions of the spirits he is channeling.

Since guardian spirits think at the same subconscious level as the person living on earth, Master Okawa can summon the spirit and find out what the person on earth is actually thinking. If the person has already returned to the other world, the spirit can give messages to the people living on earth through Master Okawa.

Since 2009, many spiritual messages have been openly recorded by Master Okawa and published. Spiritual messages from the guardian spirits of people living today such as Donald Trump, former Japanese Prime Minister Shinzo Abe and Chinese President Xi Jinping, as well as spiritual messages sent from the spirit world by Jesus Christ, Muhammad, Thomas Edison, Mother Teresa, Steve Jobs and Nelson Mandela are just a tiny pack of spiritual messages that were published so far.

Domestically, in Japan, these spiritual messages are being read by a wide range of politicians and mass media, and the high-level contents of these books are delivering an impact even more on politics, news and public opinion. In recent years, there have been spiritual messages recorded in English, and

English translations are being done on the spiritual messages given in Japanese. These have been published overseas, one after another, and have started to shake the world.

1. The guardian spirit / spirit in the other world...

2. Goes inside Master Okawa in this world

3. Master Okawa speaks the words of the guardian spirit / spirit

For more about spiritual messages and a complete list of books in the Spiritual Interview Series, visit okawabooks.com

ABOUT HAPPY SCIENCE

Happy Science is a global movement that empowers individuals to find purpose and spiritual happiness and to share that happiness with their families, societies, and the world. With more than 12 million members around the world, Happy Science aims to increase awareness of spiritual truths and expand our capacity for love, compassion, and joy so that together we can create the kind of world we all wish to live in.

Activities at Happy Science are based on the Principle of Happiness (Love, Wisdom, Self-Reflection, and Progress). This principle embraces worldwide philosophies and beliefs, transcending boundaries of culture and religions.

Love teaches us to give ourselves freely without expecting anything in return; it encompasses giving, nurturing, and forgiving.

Wisdom leads us to the insights of spiritual truths, and opens us to the true meaning of life and the will of God (the universe, the highest power, Buddha).

Self-Reflection brings a mindful, nonjudgmental lens to our thoughts and actions to help us find our truest selves—the essence of our souls—and deepen our connection to the highest power. It helps us attain a clean and peaceful mind and leads us to the right life path.

Progress emphasizes the positive, dynamic aspects of our spiritual growth—actions we can take to manifest and spread happiness around the world. It's a path that not only expands our soul growth, but also furthers the collective potential of the world we live in.

PROGRAMS AND EVENTS

The doors of Happy Science are open to all. We offer a variety of programs and events, including self-exploration and self-growth programs, spiritual seminars, meditation and contemplation sessions, study groups, and book events.

Our programs are designed to:
* Deepen your understanding of your purpose and meaning in life
* Improve your relationships and increase your capacity to love unconditionally
* Attain peace of mind, decrease anxiety and stress, and feel positive
* Gain deeper insights and a broader perspective on the world
* Learn how to overcome life's challenges
  ... and much more.

For more information, visit happy-science.org.

CONTACT INFORMATION

Happy Science is a worldwide organization with branches and temples around the globe. For a comprehensive list, visit the worldwide directory at *happy-science.org*. The following are some of the many Happy Science locations:

UNITED STATES AND CANADA

New York
79 Franklin St., New York, NY 10013, USA
Phone: 1-212-343-7972
Fax: 1-212-343-7973
Email: ny@happy-science.org
Website: happyscience-usa.org

New Jersey
66 Hudson St., #2R, Hoboken, NJ 07030, USA
Phone: 1-201-313-0127
Email: nj@happy-science.org
Website: happyscience-usa.org

Chicago
2300 Barrington Rd., Suite #400,
Hoffman Estates, IL 60169, USA
Phone: 1-630-937-3077
Email: chicago@happy-science.org
Website: happyscience-usa.org

Florida
5208 8th St., Zephyrhills, FL 33542, USA
Phone: 1-813-715-0000
Fax: 1-813-715-0010
Email: florida@happy-science.org
Website: happyscience-usa.org

Atlanta
1874 Piedmont Ave., NE Suite 360-C
Atlanta, GA 30324, USA
Phone: 1-404-892-7770
Email: atlanta@happy-science.org
Website: happyscience-usa.org

San Francisco
525 Clinton St.
Redwood City, CA 94062, USA
Phone & Fax: 1-650-363-2777
Email: sf@happy-science.org
Website: happyscience-usa.org

Los Angeles
1590 E. Del Mar Blvd., Pasadena, CA 91106, USA
Phone: 1-626-395-7775
Fax: 1-626-395-7776
Email: la@happy-science.org
Website: happyscience-usa.org

Orange County
16541 Gothard St. Suite 104
Huntington Beach, CA 92647
Phone: 1-714-659-1501
Email: oc@happy-science.org
Website: happyscience-usa.org

San Diego
7841 Balboa Ave. Suite #202
San Diego, CA 92111, USA
Phone: 1-626-395-7775
Fax: 1-626-395-7776
E-mail: sandiego@happy-science.org
Website: happyscience-usa.org

Hawaii
Phone: 1-808-591-9772
Fax: 1-808-591-9776
Email: hi@happy-science.org
Website: happyscience-usa.org

Kauai
3343 Kanakolu Street, Suite 5
Lihue, HI 96766, USA
Phone: 1-808-822-7007
Fax: 1-808-822-6007
Email: kauai-hi@happy-science.org
Website: happyscience-usa.org

Toronto
845 The Queensway
Etobicoke, ON M8Z 1N6, Canada
Phone: 1-416-901-3747
Email: toronto@happy-science.org
Website: happy-science.ca

Vancouver
#201-2607 East 49th Avenue,
Vancouver, BC, V5S 1J9, Canada
Phone: 1-604-437-7735
Fax: 1-604-437-7764
Email: vancouver@happy-science.org
Website: happy-science.ca

INTERNATIONAL

Tokyo
1-6-7 Togoshi, Shinagawa,
Tokyo, 142-0041, Japan
Phone: 81-3-6384-5770
Fax: 81-3-6384-5776
Email: tokyo@happy-science.org
Website: happy-science.org

Seoul
74, Sadang-ro 27-gil,
Dongjak-gu, Seoul, Korea
Phone: 82-2-3478-8777
Fax: 82-2-3478-9777
Email: korea@happy-science.org
Website: happyscience-korea.org

London
3 Margaret St.
London, W1W 8RE United Kingdom
Phone: 44-20-7323-9255
Fax: 44-20-7323-9344
Email: eu@happy-science.org
Website: www.happyscience-uk.org

Taipei
No. 89, Lane 155, Dunhua N. Road,
Songshan District, Taipei City 105, Taiwan
Phone: 886-2-2719-9377
Fax: 886-2-2719-5570
Email: taiwan@happy-science.org
Website: happyscience-tw.org

Sydney
516 Pacific Highway, Lane Cove North,
2066 NSW, Australia
Phone: 61-2-9411-2877
Fax: 61-2-9411-2822
Email: sydney@happy-science.org

Kuala Lumpur
No 22A, Block 2, Jalil Link Jalan Jalil
Jaya 2, Bukit Jalil 57000,
Kuala Lumpur, Malaysia
Phone: 60-3-8998-7877
Fax: 60-3-8998-7977
Email: malaysia@happy-science.org
Website: happyscience.org.my

Sao Paulo
Rua. Domingos de Morais 1154,
Vila Mariana, Sao Paulo SP
CEP 04010-100, Brazil
Phone: 55-11-5088-3800
Email: sp@happy-science.org
Website: happyscience.com.br

Kathmandu
Kathmandu Metropolitan City,
Ward No. 15, Ring Road, Kimdol,
Sitapaila Kathmandu, Nepal
Phone: 977-1-427-2931
Email: nepal@happy-science.org

Jundiai
Rua Congo, 447, Jd. Bonfiglioli
Jundiai-CEP, 13207-340, Brazil
Phone: 55-11-4587-5952
Email: jundiai@happy-science.org

Kampala
Plot 877 Rubaga Road, Kampala
P.O. Box 34130 Kampala, UGANDA
Phone: 256-79-4682-121
Email: uganda@happy-science.org

ABOUT HAPPINESS REALIZATION PARTY

The Happiness Realization Party (HRP) was founded in May 2009 by Master Ryuho Okawa as part of the Happy Science Group. HRP strives to improve the Japanese society, based on three basic political principles of "freedom, democracy, and faith," and let Japan promote individual and public happiness from Asia to the world as a leader nation.

1) Diplomacy and Security: Protecting Freedom, Democracy, and Faith of Japan and the World from China's Totalitarianism

Japan's current defense system is insufficient against China's expanding hegemony and the threat of North Korea's nuclear missiles. Japan, as the leader of Asia, must strengthen its defense power and promote strategic diplomacy together with the nations which share the values of freedom, democracy, and faith. Further, HRP aims to realize world peace under the leadership of Japan, the nation with the spirit of religious tolerance.

2) Economy: Early economic recovery through utilizing the "wisdom of the private sector"

Economy has been damaged severely by the novel coronavirus originated in China. Many companies have been forced into bankruptcy or out of business. What is needed for economic recovery now is not subsidies and regulations by the government, but policies which can utilize the "wisdom of the private sector."

For more information, visit en.hr-party.jp

HAPPY SCIENCE ACADEMY JUNIOR AND SENIOR HIGH SCHOOL

Happy Science Academy Junior and Senior High School is a boarding school founded with the goal of educating the future leaders of the world who can have a big vision, persevere, and take on new challenges.

Currently, there are two campuses in Japan; the Nasu Main Campus in Tochigi Prefecture, founded in 2010, and the Kansai Campus in Shiga Prefecture, founded in 2013.

Nasu Main Campus

Kansai Campus

ABOUT HS PRESS

HS Press is an imprint of IRH Press Co., Ltd. IRH Press Co., Ltd., based in Tokyo, was founded in 1987 as a publishing division of Happy Science. IRH Press publishes religious and spiritual books, journals, magazines and also operates broadcast and film production enterprises. For more information, visit *okawabooks.com*.

Follow us on:

f Facebook: Okawa Books   🅞 Instagram: OkawaBooks

▶ Youtube: Okawa Books   🐦 Twitter: Okawa Books

𝓟 Pinterest: Okawa Books   g Goodreads: Ryuho Okawa

——— **NEWSLETTER** ———

To receive book related news, promotions and events, please subscribe to our newsletter below.

🔗 eepurl.com/bsMeJj

 ——— **AUDIO / VISUAL MEDIA** ———

YOUTUBE   **PODCAST**

Introduction of Ryuho Okawa's titles; topics ranging from self-help, current affairs, spirituality, religion, and the universe.

BOOKS BY RYUHO OKAWA

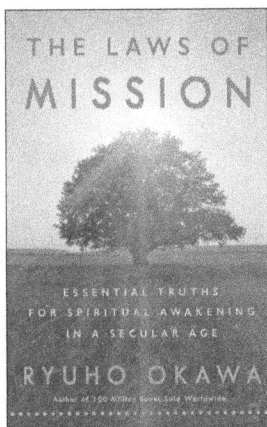

THE LAWS OF MISSION

ESSENTIAL TRUTHS FOR SPIRITUAL AWAKENING IN A SECULAR AGE

In this day and age of advanced scientific and information technology, we are often deluded by a false sense that we know everything. But in fact, many people cannot even answer simple but fundamental questions about life, such as "what's the purpose of our life" and "what happens after death."

In this book, Ryuho Okawa offers integral spiritual truths that bring about spiritual awakening within each of us. This book helps us find the purpose and meaning of our life and make the right decisions so that we can walk on the path to happiness.

For a complete list of books, visit okawabooks.com

the Laws of
JUSTICE

How We Can Solve World Conflicts & Bring Peace

How can we resolve conflicts in this world? There are two major trends opposing each other in the world today. One center around the United States. This force is comprised of countries that want to support and spread the ideologies of democracy, liberalism, fundamental human rights and market economies. The other is a force comprised of countries that will suffer if these ideologies spread across the world, because their ways of thinking and methods differ. There is a battle between these two forces. *(continued inside)*

RYUHO OKAWA
Author of 100 Million Books Sold Worldwide

THE LAWS OF JUSTICE
HOW WE CAN SOLVE
WORLD CONFLICTS & BRING PEACE

How can we solve conflicts in this world? Why is it that we continue to live in a world of turmoil, when we all wish to live in a world of peace and harmony?

In recent years, we've faced issues that jeopardize international peace and security, including the rise of ISIS, Syrian civil war and refugee crisis, break-off of diplomatic relations between Saudi Arabia and Iran, Russia's annexation of Crimea, China's military expansion, and North Korea's nuclear development.

This book shows what global justice is from a comprehensive perspective of the Supreme God. Becoming aware of this view will let us embrace differences in beliefs, recognize other people's divine nature, and love and forgive one another. It will also become the key to solving the issues we face, whether they're religious, political, societal, economic, or academic, and help the world become a better and safer world for all of us living today.

For a complete list of books, visit okawabooks.com

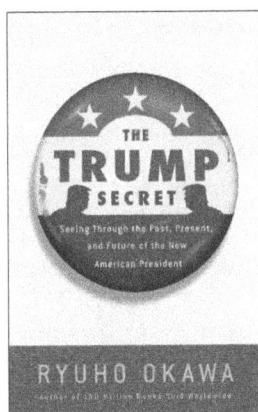

THE TRUMP SECRET

Seeing Through the Past, Present, and Future
of the New American President

Donald Trump's victory in the 2016 presidential election surprised almost all major vote forecasters who predicted Hillary Clinton's victory. But 10 months earlier, in January 2016, Ryuho Okawa, Global Visionary, a renowned spiritual leader, and international best-selling author, had already foreseen Trump's victory. This book contains a series of lectures and interviews that unveil the secrets to Trump's victory and makes predictions of what will happen under his presidency. This book predicts the coming of a new America that will go through a great transformation from the "red and blue states" to the United States.

Contents

For a complete list of books, visit okawabooks.com

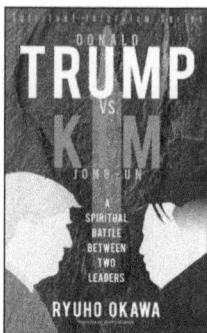

DONALD TRUMP VS. KIM JONG-UN

A SPIRITUAL BATTLE BETWEEN TWO LEADERS

Who will pull the trigger first, Kim Jong-un or Donald Trump? The North Korean issue is entering the final phase. This book tells Kim Jong-un's scenario and the crucial points of Donald Trump's strategy. Here is the top-secret information to the North Korean issue.

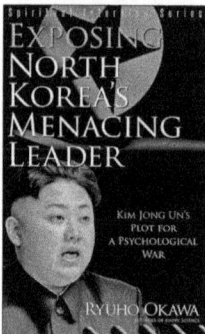

EXPOSING NORTH KOREA'S MENACING LEADER

KIM JONG UN'S PLOT FOR A PSYCHOLOGICAL WAR

This book reveals the role that North Korea is playing in China's imperialistic strategy and the two nations' close ties with Iran. Together, China and Kim Jong Un are carrying out a psychological war that takes full advantage of the weaknesses of Japanese Prime Minister Abe and United States President Obama.

SPIRITUAL INTERVIEW WITH THE GUARDIAN SPIRIT OF NEW SOUTH KOREAN PRESIDENT MOON JAE-IN

THE TRUE INTENTIONS BEHIND HIS KOREAN UNIFICATION

This book has three chapters, one of which is the spiritual interview with President Moon Jae-in, and subsequent one which reveals his past life. Read this book to find out. It is precious material in predicting the future events.

For a complete list of books, visit okawabooks.com

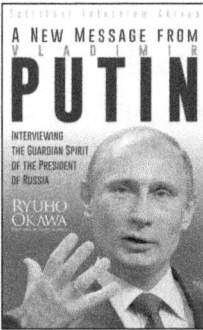

A New Message From Vladimir Putin

Inverviewing the Guardian Spirit of the President of Russia

We hereby bring you the spiritual message from the guardian spirit of President Putin, the politician who is the center of attention of not just the people of Russia but of the whole world, regardless of it being in a good or a bad way. In the Preface, it says, "President Putin's true intentions, which are 90 percent misunderstood."

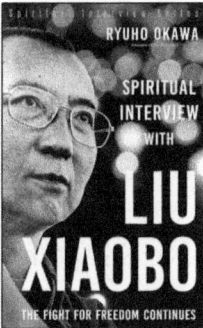

Spiritual Interview with Liu Xiaobo

The Fight for Freedom Continues

On July 21, 2017, 8 days after his death, the spirit of Liu Xiaobo was resurrected to deliver his messages. This book reveals the truths about China, a totalitarian country that doesn't grant freedom to its people. In this book, the Chinese Nobel Prize winner shares his wish to hand down the movement of China's democratization to future generations.

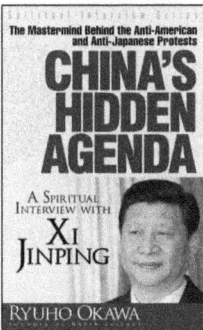

China's Hidden Agenda

The Mastermind Behind the Anti-American and Anti-Japanese Protests

"I wanted to stir up the anti-American movement in the Arab world to make sure that the United States won't be able to attack Syria or Iran...I'm the mastermind behind the Muhammad video."

—Xi Jinping's Guardian Spirit

For a complete list of books, visit okawabooks.com

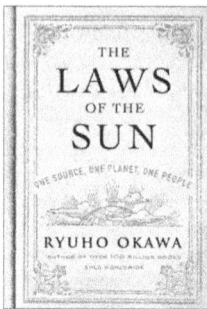

THE LAWS OF THE SUN
ONE SOURCE, ONE PLANET, ONE PEOPLE

IMAGINE IF YOU COULD ASK GOD why He created this world and what spiritual laws He used to shape us—and everything around us. If we could understand His designs and intentions, we could discover what our goals in life should be and whether our actions move us closer to those goals or farther away.

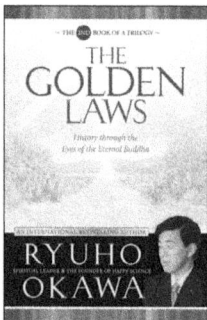

THE GOLDEN LAWS
HISTORY THROUGH THE EYES OF THE ETERNAL BUDDHA

The Golden Laws reveals how Buddha's Plan has been unfolding on earth, and outlines five thousand years of the secret history of humankind. Once we understand the true course of history, we cannot help but become aware of the significance of our spiritual mission in the present age.

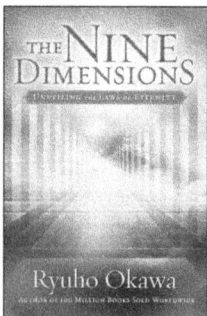

THE NINE DIMENSIONS
UNVEILING THE LAWS OF ETERNITY

This book is a window into the mind of our loving God, who encourages us to grow into greater angels. It reveals His deepest intentions, answering the timely question of why He conceived such a colorful medley of religions, philosophies, sciences, arts, and other forms of expression.

For a complete list of books, visit okawabooks.com

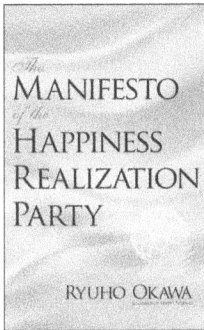

THE MANIFESTO OF THE HAPPINESS REALIZATION PARTY

This book is a historical declaration to change the world through a peaceful revolution by the philosophy and speech based on the Truth, rather than by violence or massacre. It also states on the assessment of the meaning of WWII as well as how the relation between religion and politics should be. It is a must read for all people who wish to build a true utopia.

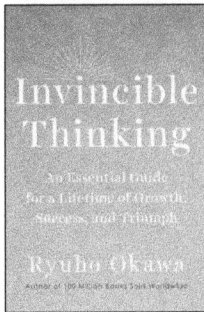

INVINCIBLE THINKING
AN ESSENTIAL GUIDE FOR A LIFETIME OF GROWTH, SUCCESS, AND TRIUMPH

In this book, Ryuho Okawa lays out the principles of invincible thinking that will allow us to achieve long-lasting triumph. This powerful and unique philosophy is not only about becoming successful or achieving our goal in life, but also about building the foundation of life that becomes the basis of our life-long, lasting success and happiness.

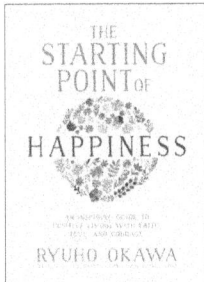

THE STARTING POINT OF HAPPINESS
AN INSPIRING GUIDE TO POSITIVE LIVING WITH FAITH, LOVE, AND COURAGE

In *The Starting Point of Happiness*, author Ryuho Okawa awakens us to the true spiritual values of our life; he beautifully illustrates, in simple but profound words, how we can find purpose and meaning in life and attain happiness that lasts forever.

For a complete list of books, visit okawabooks.com

www.ingramcontent.com/pod-product-compliance
Lightning Source LLC
Chambersburg PA
CBHW032056020426
42335CB00011B/370